FESTIVALS OF
EUROPE

Festivals of
Europe

By
GORDON COOPER

1961

PERCIVAL MARSHALL
LONDON

ACKNOWLEDGMENTS

In the preparation of this book I must first thank Miss Sylvie Nickels for her considerable and invaluable assistance. Her own wide knowledge has contributed considerably to the information given for several countries. Next, there is Dr. Giulio Tobino who has checked the chapter covering Italy, while Mr. Vivian Rowe has given similar assistance for France, Herr von Koningsbruggen for Holland, Dr. Jordan and Major W. Ingham for Austria. Many of the photos have come from the respective national tourist offices in London, to all of whom I am indebted.

Printed in Great Britain by the Electrical Press Ltd., Maidenhead, and published by Percival Marshall and Co. Ltd., 19-20, Noel Street, London, W.1.

Contents

Introduction

WHENEVER I GO ON A HOLIDAY, I LIKE TO HAVE A DEFINITE objective. I think many other people feel the same. Too often nowadays tourists have to follow an itinerary that is not their own choice. They are conducted in guided parties round the sights, but usually rather hurriedly. How much pleasanter it is, though, to be master of one's own time and be free to linger according to one's own inclinations.

This book aims, therefore, at telling you about the many interesting festivals held each year throughout Europe. They are connected with religious events, sports, carnivals, traditional celebrations of all kinds, agricultural and horticultural shows, trade fairs, and wine and gastronomic festivities.

The book covers 25 countries, and the various events are usually tabulated in sections, each following a similar plan. Sometimes, however, it has not been possible to differentiate between sections, for an event marked down under " traditional " may well be considered as coming under " religion." But I have endeavoured to make the layout as lucid as I can. Again, it is not always possible to give exact dates for a festival, for they change from year to year. You can easily, however, find out what's on by writing to the respective tourist information office in London for their current " Calendar of Events."

This book is the product of my own frequent journeys in every country in Europe. I do not claim, of course, to have attended all the festivals described—that would be almost an impossible feat in a single lifetime—but I have been to many of them, and certainly to all those of outstanding importance. To help the reader, I have marked certain festivals with an asterisk; this is an indication that it is an outstanding event of its kind and merits a special visit.

I am always glad to have readers' letters containing advice or criticism, for it is hardly possible to be infallible, although I have taken every step to be accurate. Obviously, too, there may be some omissions, but none, I think, of great importance.

CHAPTER ONE

A Choice of Festivals

YOUR CHOICE OF A FESTIVAL MAY WELL HINGE ON THE FACT
that you will be in a certain neighbourhood on a date when a traditional
event is taking place. On the other hand, you may well want to plan
your holiday to coincide with something you especially wish to see. This
is particularly the case with musical festivals. I am not going to say that
any one of these is better than another, for a taste in music is purely a
personal affair. I suppose most experts would agree that Bayreuth,
Salzburg and Edinburgh festivals are among the leading ones in Europe,
but some of the others on the international list offer great appeal, often
because of the surroundings in which they are held. To listen to a
tragedy in the ancient theatre of Epidaurus, to listen to Mozart in the
open-air auditorium of the Archbishop's Palace in Aix-en-Provence, and
to look on ballet danced in the superb gardens of the Generalife in
Granada, are just three examples providing memorable experiences.

Then, there are certain events which only occur at lengthy intervals:
the Passion Play at Oberammergau, each tenth year, and the Festival
of the Vignerons, Vevey, every twenty-fifth year. Neither should be
missed, when occasion offers. But I think my own especial favourite is
the Pageant of the Holy Blood in Bruges (every fifth year, 1962, 1967,
etc.), which I have already attended twice and will do so again.

Among the great religious festivals, I think that Holy Week in Spain
must come first, although I would prefer to recommend some other city
than Seville, the most famous centre. The Feast of Corpus Christi ranks
almost equal in spectacular importance. Again, there is the Feast of
St. James in Santiago de Compostela which well repays any pilgrim's
journey. Another religious celebration which remains in my memory
is that of St. Nicholas at Bari. Then, for strict pilgrimages, Lourdes
comes first, with Fatima a close second in popular appeal.

It is not easy to be selective over traditional secular events. The
" Fallas " at Valencia are too noisy for my liking, and that goes too for
the Piedigrotta in Naples. But what is rejoicing without lots of noise ?
If your fancy turns to the jollity of Carnival, there are those at Nice and
Viareggio, both well publicised and colourful, while the various towns
and villages of Catholic Rhineland and Bavaria (especially Munich)
maintain rounds of gaiety for several weeks, culminating usually with

3

elaborate processions on Rose Monday, just prior to the start of Lent. Mention must also be made of Carnival observances in Maastricht (Holland) and in Binche (Belgium) which features elaborately dressed mummers called *Gilles*.

Among the historical celebrations, I think everyone should at some time in their life attend Il Palio in Siena, the Sardinian Cavalcade at Sassari, the Princely Wedding in Landshut, and the Great Gilles Carnival in Binche (already mentioned). But there are so many fascinating occasions that I find it hard to be selective. What fun, for instance, I had at the Fête of the Tarasque in Tarascon, while there is rather a similar kind of affair at Fürth-im-Wald in northern Bavaria.

Wine festivals are always jolly affairs, with everyone joining in, and here it is hard to beat some of the Rhineland villages. And France, too, has its gay celebrations.

From a perusal of this book you will note that Great Britain, Italy, Spain, France and Germany probably lead in the number and variety of their traditional events. Do not, however, ignore Belgium which is amazingly rich in its celebrations, many of them unique of their kind. I think, perhaps, that your chief joy may come from encountering some festival I have missed, thus making your own personal discovery—one of the joys of travel, just like finding out a small restaurant or hotel where you enjoy a superb meal but which is not listed in any of the gastronomic guides.

CHAPTER TWO

Some Travel Hints

1. When intending to visit a festival enquire at the National Tourist Office in London of the country concerned whether it is necessary to book seats in advance; also for room accommodation. Often, if the latter is strained, you will find that you can get in at a nearby town or village and travel to and from the festival by public transport. In some cases, a reliable travel agent can help you in this essential matter.

2. It is often feasible to secure seats on the spot, even though they may, apparently, be sold out in advance. But, beware of touts; and it is recommended that you get advice and possibly practical help from the local tourist information office. In some cases, too, the management of your hotel can assist.

3. When booking seats for a festival study the sun, for it is most unpleasant to have to sit on a very hot day through a show with the sun beating into your eyes. This is particularly to be noted in the case of bullfights, where those seats with backs to the sun or in the shade naturally command higher prices.

4. In opera-houses and theatres be careful not to get a seat from which you are unable to see the stage properly. Back seats, for instance, in the side boxes should often be refused because of this disadvantage. Beware also of the *strapontin*, a folding seat attached to an aisle chair, usually with no back; occupants must continually get up to let people through the aisle. In many open-air performances the seating consists of stone seats. It is advisable to take or hire some cushion on which to sit.

5. If you do not understand the language of the theatrical performance buy a book of words beforehand with an English text. They are usually on sale and increase considerably your enjoyment.

6. Before taking your seat it is advisable to find out where the toilets are situated, and, incidentally, to learn the differing signs for *Gentlemen* and *Ladies*.

7. Beware of taking young children to any lengthy performance, for they are apt to get bored and possibly embarrassing.

8. In a city, always carry a street-map in your pocket; and make sure you know the name and address of your hotel or room—otherwise you may get " lost." Write the name down in capital letters on a card, for it is useful to show a cabman or taxi-driver.

9.   If attending a wine or other joyous festival it is sensible to take a couple of Alka-Seltzers before going to bed. They prevent any hangover feeling the next morning. Aspirins, too, can be useful.

10.   At drinking festivities, remember to eat occasionally and, above all, try not to mix your drinks too much.

11.   Take a vacuum flask with you. It keeps cold drinks cold as well as hot drinks hot. In the hot weather you can spend a lot of money otherwise on buying cold drinks. Some glucose sweets, too, are excellent should you get exhausted, as are also face cleansing pads, such as " Quickies."

12.   If attending a performance after dark it may possibly get chilly, so carry a light woolly with you; also a light mac, for thunderstorms can occur.

13.   Take ear-plugs with you, for the streets can be noisy during festival time, and even the most lively person requires some sleep. If going to an evening performance it is wise (if not so young) to take an afternoon siesta beforehand, otherwise you may, like me, find yourself nodding and even snoring during the show !

14.   Keep cool by carrying a cheap fan. I always take one with me abroad and have no qualms at being considered odd (but sensible) by using it.

15.   An air cushion that can also be used as a bag is a useful article to include in your luggage.

16.   Don't forget to carry your own soap, for it is rarely obtainable abroad in any but the first-class hotels.

17.   If you suffer from " nervy " feet, take a pair of light slippers with you. I wear them on all occasions when I am likely to be seated for some time.

18.   In most countries abroad queueing for buses and trams is un-known, and it is a case of fighting to get on. For this reason, especially with ladies and children, it is best to hire a cab, enquiring first about the price to your destination.

19.   Mosquitoes and midges may be trying when you are at an open-air performance; take something, therefore, with you to overcome the irritating bites.

20.   Learn the phrases for " Good morning," " Thank you," and " Please," for courtesy always pays.

21.   When travelling abroad, always keep in mind these three Golden Rules:

(i) Do not allow petty irritations to upset your equanimity.

(ii) Do not waste time seeing things which do not interest you.

(iii) Do not become over-exhausted through over-sightseeing. Far better to take things more easily, especially if you are no longer young, and relax.

22. Finally, here are some useful tips for holiday photography prepared by the Photographic Information Council.

Tips for holiday photography

Today, no family goes on holiday without a camera. Many take two—one for still and one for movie.

Except for items 11, 13, 15, 17 and 18, all hints are appropriate for still and cine photography.

1. Make a pre-holiday camera check to make sure that everything is working perfectly. Better to find any defects now than when on holiday in some remote village.
2. When going abroad, take your sales receipt or valid insurance certificate to prove to British customs officers that the camera was purchased in this country and that duty and purchase tax have been paid.
3. Check that your camera insurance policy covers foreign travel, if you are going abroad.
4. Stock up on film. Even in this country, shops in small villages may not stock your favourite brand, particularly in colour, and when going abroad you will find that prices are generally higher than they are in this country.
5. On the beach remember to close down the lens by $\frac{1}{2}$ or 1 f stop to prevent over-exposure.
6. Use an ultra-violet filter with colour film while in the mountains to prevent excessive bluishness.
7. On the beach always keep a filter on your camera to protect the lens from blowing sand and salt spray. An ultra-violet filter is excellent for colour and requires no exposure compensation. A very light yellow filter can be used with black and white film and also helps to accentuate the clouds.
8. For family snaps, keep the stiffly posed photographs at a minimum. Concentrate on getting candid shots of the family at play.
9. When going abroad, don't concentrate exclusively on landscapes— no matter how pretty they are. Photograph the local residents, particularly if they are in picturesque costume. Get close-up when photographing people.
10. When taking portraits try to place your subject in the shade. Direct sunlight not only causes your subject to squint but gives unflattering, heavy shadows.
11. Make full use of your flashgun on holiday—indoors, and outdoors after dark.
12. Shoot pictures at dusk or after dark by time exposure to capture the illuminations of the resort you are staying at.

13. Use the delayed action of your camera frequently so that you can " get in the picture."

14. Be sure to use a lens hood whenever you are shooting into the sun. This often makes for very effective photographs and a lens hood costs only a few shillings.

15. When you return from holiday, make a day-by-day pictorial album of all the things you did. You will appreciate it during the winter months.

16. Do not keep your camera and/or film in the boot or glove compartment of your car. These very quickly get very hot on a sunny day, and heat is a major enemy of both film and cameras.

17. When taking movies, make sure that you make each scene long enough so the audience can grasp what is going on. Movie scenes should average between eight and ten seconds in length.

18. When " panning " a movie camera, make sure that it is done *slowly* and smoothly. Do not pan unless absolutely necessary. Often the scene can be photographed better by taking several " straight " shots.

CHAPTER THREE

Austria

AUSTRIA HAS MANY GIFTS TO OFFER THOSE SEEKING TO LEARN about her characteristic festivals. And when you go there to seek the banquet of the soul that waits you, there are many other rewards to be discovered when you mingle with perhaps the most friendly people in Europe. The country has, in fact, a delightful personality, so well expressed by that untranslatable word *gemütlich*, which expresses various admirable human traits, such as cheerfulness, jollity, easy going companionship. All these things contribute very much to the full enjoyment of a holiday. And almost the year round there is something of traditional entertainment for you to enjoy.

CARNIVALS

Carnival, or *Fasching*, is celebrated generally all over Austria. The climax of the Vienna Carnival Season is the Opera Ball, a magnificent formal affair; other formal balls include the " Ball of the Vienna Philharmonic " in the Musikvereins-Sâle and the " Techniker Cercle " (the Ball of the Industries), also the Lawyers' Ball, while there is the traditional " Fools' Night," which takes place on Shrove Sunday. Especially delightful are the Rosenmontag-Redoute on Shrove Monday, the jolly Spektakelfeste (fancy-dress balls), and the various Herring Banquets on Ash Wednesday.

Curious carnival customs are observed in the small Tyrolean towns of Imst, Thaur, Telfs and Nassereith. Those partaking in the ceremony, known as the " Schemenlaufen," wear horrific wooden masks; this was originally a ritual dance for driving out the demons of winter. These grimacing masks, by the way, are often prized heirlooms, and some of the participants wear decorated head-dresses. There is much noise and shouting, as well as dancing and singing in the streets. This particular celebration, however, does not take place every year—usually, every fourth year, but there is a customary arrangement between Imst, Telfs and Thaur—all in the Upper Inn Valley—to arrange their Carnivals in different years, so as not to clash with each other. At Telfs, there is the **Schleicherlaufen,** when 17 groups of mummers, fantastically dressed, symbolise an ancient custom in the change of seasons as well as humorous parodies of recent events. Then, at Thaur (near Innsbruck), there is a

9

procession called the **Thaurer Mulln,** a pageant of local importance with the traditional mummers ringing bells, cracking whips and playing tricks on the onlookers.

The Nassereith **Schellerlaufen** is an extremely interesting carnival custom, and is also rooted in pagan rites. The performers are all local boys, in whose families the individual " parts " have been handed down for generations. The Nassereith ceremony is related to the **Glöckler-laufen** to be seen at Stainach (Styria) and whose performers wear big tinsel stars as head-dresses. Again at Axams (Tyrol) it is the jolly **Wampelreiter** who parade through the village on Candlemas Day, preceded by the " Schneuzeltücheltuxer " cracking their whips. The latter lead off the noisy round that is supposed to drive out the winter demons.

Perhaps as attractive a centre as any in Austria for the ordinary visitor would be Salzburg. Here they have age-old traditions for their Fasching Weeks. There are fancy-dress balls with folk-dancing and folk-songs, operettas, special concerts. Furthermore, special trips are arranged to the nearby Gastein Valley for the **Perchten Run** (on skis), and to the Wolfgangsee for the **" Dreikönigs Ride."** A great number of winter sports events are held in fancy dress—a carnival, in fact, on skis—and visitors will find the programme light-hearted and gay.

CULTURAL

Mozart was born in Salzburg, and although he was, according to his own account, unhappy in this lovely city, yet he is commemorated each year at the famous **Salzburg Festival** which takes place from the end of July to the end of August. Performances are given in various places, including the magnificent new " Festspielhaus " (Festival Theatre) which is as modernly equipped as any in Europe. There are other entertainments in Salzburg during this summer festival, including performances of Hugo von Hofmannsthal's " Everyman " which are given in the Cathedral Square. And there are the famous puppet shows given in the Marionette Theatre—a real joy, for there is nothing better of its kind elsewhere. An international folklore festival week is held after the Salzburg Festival. Another musical treat in this gracious city is **Musical Spring** when from the end of May until early June there is a little festival of Viennese classical music. Many of the concerts are given in historic buildings such as the Residenz and Mirabell palace. As accommodation is limited, tickets should be ordered well in advance. And there are musical occasions at other times of the year.

The **Vienna Festival** offers a daily choice of ten or more performances at festival time (end of May to end of June). The opera house, completely rebuilt since the war, is one of the most magnificent in Europe. The musical tradition of Vienna, too, draws the best performers in a repertoire

embracing classical and romantic as well as contemporary music. Vienna
is also the recognised capital of operetta; and there are excellent performances of straight plays. In fact, you will be unlucky if you should
visit Vienna and find it barren of musical fare. Worth noting are the
Sound and Light performances during the summer in the park at the
Belvedere Palace.

Linz has its annual **Bruckner Festival** during the first week of July,
with performances in St. Florian's, the church where the composer was
organist and where he is buried. Eisenstadt offers, annually, Haydn
memorial concerts (sometimes also in Rohrau, the composer's birthplace). Note, too, that in this capital of Burgenland there is the composer's home, now a Haydn Museum. Graz, the capital of Styria.
has a festival every year, with a wide programme of operas, concerts and
plays—it is held from mid-June to the first week in July. Then, an unusual
kind of event is the **Bregenz Festival,** held from the last week in July to
the third week in August. In this case, an operetta and ballet are performed on a floating stage on Lake Constance, while dramas and concerts
are given in the local theatre and in the Stadthalle; also, on occasion, at
nearby Feldkirch. The performances are first-class, but my previous
travel hint regarding midges should be noted for the open-air performances. At Baden, near Vienna, operetta performances are given
in the open-air theatre during July and August.

A similar kind of **Lake Festival** is held at Mörbisch on the Neusiedler
See (Burgenland), taking place during August. There are performances
of operettas on a stage constructed in a reedy cove. Performances are
always given on Saturdays and Sundays; and special buses provide the
connection with Vienna.

Among the smaller drama festivals, the small Carinthian walled town
of Friesach offers one during the summer, and it is staged in the courtyard
of the local castle. There is pleasant inn accommodation available, or you
could arrange to lodge in nearby Klagenfurt. Also to be noted are the
Castle Plays in Forchtenstein (Burgenland), end June to end July
(Saturdays and Sundays).

Should you be in Innsbruck during the summer it is possible you
may be able to witness a most delightful performance at the famous
Goldenes Dachl (Golden Roof) in the old town. Here, on the outside
balcony, the Wilten Band and Boy Singers provide an open-air concert,
while on other occasions there is a Trumpet Fanfare. It is a truly enchanting spectacle. Every village in Tyrol, of course, has its own band,
with the bandsmen dressed in their medieval costumes, which plays on
any special festival day. There is also usually a grand gathering of all
these bands in Innsbruck in the autumn, when they all proudly perform:
a quite fascinating and colourful sight. Worth noting, too, are the
recitals on the renowned Renaissance organ in the Silver Chapel in the

Innsbruck Hofburg. These performances on the 400-year-old instrument take place by candlelight. They are held every Wednesday from 8 p.m. to 9 p.m. from the end of June until the end of September. The illumination by candles during recitals accentuates the architectural beauty of this famous building.

Other interesting events in Tyrol include the annual commemoration honouring Andreas Hofer's memory—he was their greatest patriot—and **Brass Music Day** all over Tyrol, held usually in mid-June.

RELIGIOUS AND TRADITIONAL EVENTS

When one thinks of **Passion Plays** one's first thought turns to Oberammergau, but many persons who have attended similar productions at either Erl or Thiersee in the Austrian Tyrol consider them to be as good, if not even better. The two neighbouring villages alternate in re-enacting the story of Christ's life, the cast consisting solely of villagers maintaining a custom which originated with a vow made over 300 years ago when the plague was rampant. In the local festival hall the village carpenter may play the part of Christ, while the modern Mary may work in a local shop and Satan in a saw-mill. Every Sunday from June to September there are performances in the village for the year. Incidentally, both these places are pleasant resorts in themselves. Another Tyrolean village presenting a Passion Play is Fulpmes. For dates of performances, enquire from the Austrian State Tourist Department in London.

St. Margarethen (Burgenland), not far from Eisenstadt, stages every few years (the next occasions will be in 1962 and 1965) a **Burgenland Passion Play.** The setting is a big quarry, with good acoustics. Roughly 260 people take part in the play, some of them amateur actors. In Lower Austria there is the new Passion Play village of Kirchschlag, where performances are given in a big, new play-house. The actors are all laymen, but their work displays a high level of artistry. Performances take place every Sunday and public holiday, and on certain Saturdays. The play is not, however, an annual event.

In many places the **Processions** held on **Corpus Christi** are picturesque. The most impressive celebrations are those held on boats on the Traunsee and Hallstättersee. In each case a decorated boat bears the Holy Sacrament across the lake, followed by a procession of boats with worshippers. And at Zederhaus, Lungau, Salzburg, there is a procession with decorated poles, called **Prangstangentragen.**

Early in May, there is the traditional **Gauder Festival** at Zell am Ziller (Tyrol) where cockfights, wrestling, folk dancing, band processions and consumption of the famous Gauder beer play their part in the general jollity.

At Solstice, as part of the **Midsummer Festival,** the villages lying beside the Danube in the Wachau place egg-shells containing oil and small lighted wicks on the waters which slowly drift downstream, forming a delightful picture.

But **Church Fairs** are celebrated in many villages, usually commemorating the foundation of the village or in honour of the local Patron Saint. On these occasions, old customs are revived and folk costumes are worn. The German name for a typical function is " Kirchweihfest "—often abbreviated to " Kirtag."

Among the many harvest festivals which offer thanks for the blessings of the past year, one of the most lavish and colourful is the **Martinsfest** in Burgenland. This is a fête in honour of St. Martin, the patron saint of the region, which is held in November. It produces many exhibitions of folklore in the picturesque villages of this countryside, as for instance in the old free town of Rust, in Oggau, Purbach, and the other well-known vine-growing villages around Lake Neusiedl. For this special occasion dancing and acting groups turn out in local costumes, and special buses are run from Vienna to the region of festivities. You will find plenty of friendship and conviviality at this particular feast.

From the middle of August until well into the autumn, the **Ranggler** season is celebrated in Salzburg province in accordance with ancient peasant traditions. At various country sports meetings in which the herdsmen and shepherds of the different Alpine pastures test their skill in wrestling, thousands of curious spectators see the victor stick the white cock's feather in his hat. Three popular villages for these festivals are Tumersbach (near Zell am See), Goldegg in Pongau, and Neukirchen on the Grossvenediger.

In Salzburg and Upper Austria, a traditional event on horseback, called **Leonhardiritt** is celebrated in early November.

The **Christmas season festivities** start early, and on the eve of St. Nicholas's Day (December 6th) the saint, in traditional uniform and a long white beard, visits many towns and villages accompanied by the Devil, whose job it is to frighten naughty children. In Mitterndorf (Styria) there is a **masked procession,** and just prior to Christmas interesting ceremonies are to be seen at Igls (near Innsbruck), with the **Christmas in the Mountains**—entry of the Christ Child, followed by a Holy Night Trumpet Serenade, and concluding with a New Year's trumpeting on December 31st. In many villages, too, the so-called **"star-singers"** wander around on January 6th (Day of the Three Magi), singing Christmas carols (or similar songs).

It was at Oberndorf (near Salzburg) that the famous Christmas carol " Silent Night, Holy Night " was written and composed, and sung for the first time in 1818. The festival is still commemorated there, also in Hallein and Wagrain, while in Vienna you can hear it played on the great organ of St. Stephen's Cathedral, with the wonderful Cathedral

Choir, not to be confused with the Viennese Boys' Choir which sings only in the Imperial Chapel (Burgkapelle) on Sunday mornings, except when they have their summer holidays, taken at Hinterbichl, a tiny hamlet in Eastern Tyrol, when they also perform.

SPORTING FIXTURES

The winter sports season plays a most important role in the economy of Austria, and to provide enjoyment and interest to the thousands of foreign skiers who come to the various resorts there is an enormous programme of events. The most important centres for these events are St. Anton, Badgastein, Saalbach, Seefeld and Kitzbühel, while the 1964 Olympic Winter Games are to be held at Innsbruck. The **Arlberg-Kandahar Race** takes place at St. Anton every fifth year—the last occasion was in 1958. The **Hahnenkamm** race is one of the most important ski-ing events, and it is held each year (mid-January) at Kitzbühel. The largest **glacier international ski race** in Europe is held at Franz-Josef-Höhe, on the Grossglockner in early June, every second year. A glance at the programme of winter sports events in Austria shows you how impossible it is to list more than the most important ones I have mentioned. I would like, however, to mention that in Vienna, at the huge Eislaufverein Rink, there are some wonderful ice-skating events to be seen. There are also exciting ice-hockey matches; and the famous Vienna Ice Revue is staged daily in the Stadthalle from Christmas to early February. Other popular Austrian winter sports are **Ice Shooting,** the Austrian variety of Curling, while the Scottish game can be enjoyed in St. Anton and Kitzbühel—all with competitions. Then there are **Ice Shooting** matches, also **Tobogganing** (to be included in the next Winter Olympics) with a famous artificial run at Imst where the European Championships are held.

Turning to summer sports, there are **sailing regattas** on the Wörthersee, also on the Attersee, Traunsee and Wolfgangsee; **tennis tournaments** at Velden, **International Golf Championships** at Vienna (Whitsun), and rowing competitions at Vienna, on side-arms of the Danube. There is also the **International Sport Festival** held in Klagenfurt, Pörtschach and Velden, usually in mid-July; the championship events include cycling, boxing, swimming, tennis and ballroom dancing.

Austria has its annual six-day cycling **Tour of Austria** about the end of June, with international participation; places of starting and ending vary, but Vienna is usually the goal.

Gliding competitions are held at one or other of the gliding grounds. This sport, incidentally, is very popular in Austria, and excellent atmospheric conditions prevail.

While hardly a sport, the regular **displays of horsemanship** given in Vienna at the Hofburg Riding School merit a mention here. This unique school of riding dates back to the sixteenth century, and it takes its name from the fact that at that time mainly Spanish horses were used for the special form of classical riding evolved. To-day, the Riding School uses Lipizzan stallions, the descendants of the former imported breed. Performances are given on Sunday mornings (with the exception of July/August and December/February), while the morning training periods are also open to the public. This particular exhibition of the art of classical riding at its best is an occasion which should not be missed. During the summer (July/August), however, the horses move to Piber (Styria) where they also give their performances.

There are many good trotting meetings at Vienna's Krieau; the **Austrian Trotting Derby** is held at the end of May, the **Austrian Derby** in early June. Apart from Vienna, horse-riding events are featured at Velden and Salzburg.

TRADE FAIRS

There are several fairs annually in Austria; many of them, however, are of a specialist nature. The general **international trade fairs** are those held in Vienna (Spring Fair in March; Autumn Fair in September); at Graz (April and October); and at Innsbruck (September). The **Sample Fair** at Dornbirn (July-August) is one of the most important textile fairs in Europe; and there is the **Austrian Timber Fair** at Klagenfurt (mid-August). Then there are the various Country Fairs which have, however, much of the character of country festivals. The most popular ones showing the local or regional economy are the " **Welser (or Rieder) Volksfest**," Upper Austria, and held one year in Wels, the next in Ried. Less important are the " **Wieselburger Volksfest** " and others in Lower Austria. Further information can be obtained from the Austrian Foreign Trade Office, 1, Hyde Park Gate, S.W.7.

WINE FESTIVALS

The **Heuriger Parties** at Grinzing, Sievering and Nussdorf—all suburbs of Vienna—are the most popular wine celebrations, but many more suburbs where wine is grown also hold them. These feasts of new wine and old song have a great tradition, dating back to the era of Josef II, son of Maria Theresia, who encouraged his people in this form of jollity in order to keep them from too much active concern about what he was doing in the political field.

At the three places named, small bushes hung outside the door indicate that the establishment is open to customers. It is the custom to take your own picnic meal along with you, although you can usually buy a snack on the spot. But the main thing is the wine and the song, a combination which when allied to congenial companions enables you to capture to the full the atmosphere of Gemütlichkeit.

Wine Festivals are also held in the autumn at Rust, Mörbisch and Oggau (Burgenland), at Baden, Gumpoldskirchen and Vöslau, and in the Wachau beside the Danube; all are important wine-growing districts. In the Wachau I would mention here only Krems, Durnstein, Spitz, Loiben, while north of Krems, an excellent wine is grown in Langenlois. Fine wines are also produced in southern Styria (Leibnitz, etc.) and wine festivals are held there too. The **opening of the new wine season** is usually celebrated on St. Martin's Day (November 11th), and it is sampled in a festive manner, to the accompaniment of a delicious, crisply roasted " Martini " goose served with a cabbage-salad or red cabbage stewed in wine—a culinary speciality. A visit to a Martinmas party, in fact, held in genial country style, provides a most pleasant memory.

An unusual **wine celebration** takes place at Klosterneuberg (near Vienna), where on St. Leopold's Day (November 15th) people, including children, take part in a traditional barrel gliding, sliding down the smooth sides of a huge barrel which holds thousands of gallons of wine. Afterwards, there is feasting and other amusements.

CHAPTER FOUR

Belgium

BELGIUM CAN PROBABLY CLAIM TO HAVE MORE CARNIVALS PER square mile than any other country in Europe. Many of them have religious or historic origins; others, while by no means lacking the traditional element, are characterised by sheer *joie de vivre*.

Nearly every town and village has its particular costumed figures symbolising the carnival spirit, sometimes laughable, sometimes grotesque, often gigantic, but always playing a prominent part in the festivities. Of all these, perhaps the Gilles de Binche are the most famous, with their huge feathered head-dresses, their rhythmic dance and sense of fun. Their carnival can be seen on Shrove Tuesday and, indeed, the pre-Lent period is a gay time in many places all over the country.

But, just as the Belgians know how to enjoy their carnival time, centuries of tradition have stirred in them a feeling for religious processions of great beauty. Many of these take place at Easter, but the greatest of all occurs in May, when the Procession of the Holy Blood unfolds through the ancient streets of Bruges. Every five years, the Passion Play of the Holy Blood in Bruges is another remarkable religious event, one of the finest in Europe.

Several very lovely Sound and Light performances are included in Belgium's cultural programme, while in the field of sport she can claim a number of important motor and motor cycle racing events, headed by the Grand Prix de Belgique at Francorchamps in June.

Throughout this chapter, it should be noted that where places have both a Dutch (Flemish) and French equivalent, the more important locally has been put first. The few exceptions are in the case of main cities such as Brussels, Bruges and Ostend, where the English spelling has been used.

AGRICULTURAL, HORTICULTURAL AND LIVESTOCK SHOWS

Ghent Floralies, * Ghent, end of April to early May every five years. A magnificent international flower show which ranks amongst the best in Europe.

Begonia Festival, Lochristi, end of August. Superb floral display. A smaller festival is held at Laarne about the same time.

CARNIVALS

Fools' Monday, Ronse (Renaix). Festivities start on the first Sunday after Epiphany and reach their hectic climax the following day when thousands of masked Bonmos (madmen for the day) pay homage to their chosen king and queen, finally storming the town amidst fanfare, song and laughter.

Hoûres Carnival, Eben-Emael, end of January. Locally, *hoûres* means anyone who is dressed up—traditionally by means of a red and black striped skirt tied round the neck and a second skirt tied round the hips, the head hooded by a red-and-white checked pillow case and the face veiled. These impressive figures, armed with broom or pig's bladder, chase the inhabitants of the town, marking any they catch with two black lines on either cheek. The versatile *hoûres* also perform masked dances and shows during which they delight in making fun of their audiences.

Shrovetide Carnivals. This peak carnival time preceding Lent is celebrated in many towns and villages all over the country. Perhaps the most spectacular are as follows:

Traditional Pageant and Carnival, Malmedy, main day: Shrove Sunday. After the traditional pageant, the streets become alive with costumed figures dressed as Haguettes, Savages, Jesters, Cobblers, Long-Noses, Long-Arms and Harlequins, who run riot amongst the onlookers, playing pranks and inciting them to join in the fun.

Carnival Procession, Aalst (Alost), main day: Shrove Sunday. Leading characters in this brilliant procession are the sober giants— Seigneur Ywein and his pretty wife, Loretta, accompanied by Major Cans, a local hero. The madcap Gilles are here, too, carrying bouquets of onions.

Rosenmontag (Rose Monday), Eupen, the day before Shrove Tuesday. Gaily coloured costumes and richly decorated cars enliven the streets as the carnival prince, the foolish Funkenkorps, enters, with his charming entourage, for a brief annual reign of glory.

Great Gilles Carnival,* Binche, main day: Shrove Tuesday, but festivities start six weeks before. Undoubtedly the most famous carnival procession in Belgium, and one of the finest and strangest to be seen in Europe. It had its origin in the " Ballet of the Incas " presented in 1540 by Mary of Hungary, Ruler of the Netherlands, in honour of Charles V, who had just conquered Peru. So deep are its roots in popular tradition that everyone, from the highest to the lowest, considers it an honour to be a " Gille " and wear the tall head-dress of ostrich feathers, the jingling bells and quaint costume as they dance tirelessly through the streets to a haunting tune. As they dance, they bombard onlookers with thousands of oranges, symbolic of the treasures of Peru. In the evening, fireworks burst in a riot of colour against the night sky.

Krakelingenworp, Throwing of Biscuits, Geraardsbergen (Grammont), Sunday after Ash Wednesday. On the summit of Oudenberg hill, religious and civic authorities have the traditional if doubtful pleasure of emptying a glass of wine containing tiny live fish. Afterwards they throw thousands of cracknel biscuits to the watching crowds. In the evening, the **Tonnekenbrand** takes place: a barrel of pitch is set alight on the hilltop and, as the people dance and sing, answering fires glow from neighbouring villages.

Bal du Rat Mort, Casino at Ostend, Saturday in mid-February. A huge carnival ball, first launched at the end of the last century by the young members of the Ostend Art and Philanthropic Circle, who named it after the Montmartre cabaret where they spent many pleasant hours.

Mid-Lent Carnival, Stavelot. Half-way through Lent, carnival time makes a come-back in no uncertain manner as the white-clad, white-masked, but red-nosed Blancs-Moussis give full rein to their high spirits with paper streamers, confetti and all the clownish mischief their fertile imaginations can think up.

Mid-Lent Carnival, Fosse. Here it is the hunchbacked Chinels who delight in playing their pranks on unwary spectators, as they dance their strange way through the streets. Peculiar feature of this dance is the way in which the Chinels stop transfixed as the music stops, starting again a moment later as if jerked by an invisible string.

Flower Battles and Pageants. Many take place during August and early September, but amongst the most important are those at St. Niklaas on the first Sunday in August; at Spa in mid-August; Blankenberge, Koksijde (Coxyde) and Mechelen (Malines) at the end of August; and Wommelgem, St. Gillis (Dendermonde) and Ghent early in September.

Opening of the Ducasse,* Ath (Aat), end of August. Giants dominate the scene once more during the great annual celebrations which begin on the Saturday with the Wedding of Goliath, after which the warrior-like giant proceeds to do battle with David the Shepherd on the market place. Apparently all ends well, for Goliath is back again on Sunday for one of the finest pageants in the country, accompanied by a giant host and chariots amidst much noisy discharge of musketry, dancing and revelry.

Lovers' Fair, Arlon (Aarlen), first Thursday in December. The giants are back again to cheer up winter days in Arlon and provide its younger citizens with a preview of spring romance. Helleschsman is the name of the 17-foot giant matchmaker who speaks and sings at the Lovers' Fair. His words should carry some weight—he certainly does at 17 stone !

CULTURAL EVENTS

Sound and Light Performances, many towns throughout Belgium, either daily or at frequent intervals through the summer, usually until the middle or end of September. Perhaps the best are to be seen at Beloeil, Bouillon, Bruges, Veurne (Furnes), Ghent, Huizingen, La Roche-en-Ardenne, Mechelen (Malines), Tournai (Doornik) and Ieper (Ypres). The performances at Ghent (with stereorama), La Roche and Tournai are particularly outstanding, both for quality and beauty of setting.

International Biennal of Poetry, Knokke, September, in years with uneven numbers.

International Sculpture Festival, Antwerp, through the summer, years with uneven numbers.

Carillon Concerts, Bruges, mid-June to end of September. During certain hours of several days a week, the quaint streets of this lovely city echo with Flemish folk tunes and classical themes as they ring out from the famous Belfry. Carillon concerts are also given at Malines and other Belgian towns.

NATIONAL OR SPECIAL DAYS/WEEKS

Whitsun Fair, Antwerp, lasting for six weeks from Whit weekend. Funfair, exhibitions, concerts.

Namur Festival, Namur, whole of July. Concerts, exhibitions, trade fair, regatta on the Meuse.

Ostend Festival, one week in July. Funfair, concerts, fireworks, rowing regatta, sailing competitions.

National Day, all over the country, July 21st. A public holiday during which most towns hold a military parade and firework display.

Great Liège Fortnight, Liège (Luik), September. Cultural and artistic festival, including pageantry and folklore.

Festival of Flanders, Ghent, September. Cultural and artistic festival.

RELIGIOUS EVENTS

Procession of the Twelve Apostles, Hoegaarden, Palm Sunday. The apostles make their way slowly through the streets to the church, escorting a statue of Jesus seated on an ass. During the church service, they leave the choir and go into the sacristy, thus symbolising the treachery of Judas and their own defection. This ceremony dates back to 1631.

The Way of the Cross,* Veurne (Furnes), at midnight on Maundy Thursday. Since 1780 this pilgrims' procession has stopped before the 18 stations of the Cross built in 1626. The distance between the different stations is said to correspond with the number of steps taken by Christ from Jerusalem to Mount Calvary, a total of 5,751.

Good Friday Processions. **Stations of the Cross** pilgrims' procession, Tournai (Doornik); pilgrimage to **Vieux bon Dieu de Tancremont** near Pepinster; **Entombment Procession,** Lessines. The latter, flanked on either side by a row of torches, presents a moving procession of mourners following the cross and bearing the body of Christ.

Blessing of the Fields, Hakendover, Easter Monday. Scores of farmers ride their carthorses round a procession of praying pilgrims as they move slowly across the fields of young corn. Tradition has it that the most flattened cornfield will yield the best harvest.

Pageant of St. Evermeire, Rutten (Russon), May 1st. A miracle play dating back to the tenth century, in which a band of brigands encircles St. Evermeire and his pilgrim companions, finally massacring them. The pageant ends with the vision of their guardian angels bearing the martyrs' palm.

Procession of the Holy Blood,* Bruges, Monday after May 2nd. More than 800 years ago, Thierry d'Alsace, Count of Flanders, returned in triumph from the Second Crusade. Valour had earned him the highest honour it was possible to bestow from Baudouin III, Patriarch of Jerusalem: he was entrusted with a phial containing a drop of the Holy Blood of Christ. Every May, the people of Bruges relive his magnificent re-entry into their city, and a superb procession unfolds along a three-mile course between kneeling, reverent crowds. This is one of the most outstanding religious processions in Europe.

Passion Play of the Holy Blood,* Bruges, every five years. I consider this moving spectacle to be of outstanding importance—perhaps the finest in Europe. This truly glorious pageant play unfolds against the backdrop of Bruges' lovely Belfry, and I shall always remember the solemnity and beauty of the occasion. The next performance will take place in 1962.

Blessing of the Forest, St. Hubert, June and November. A procession of huntsmen and hornblowers is followed by a religious ceremony at the edge of the forest.

Blessing of the Sea, Ostend, end of June. A moving religious ceremony is held before an altar erected on the main promenade, during which the sea, fishing fleet and naval units receive blessing. Fishermen form a procession through the streets of the town. Similar ceremonies on a smaller scale are held at other places on the coast, such as Koksijde (Coxyde), Blankenberge, Wenduine, La Panne and Heist-Duinbergen, during the summer.

Procession of the Penitents, Veurne (Furnes), last Sunday of July. For more than 300 years this pilgrimage has retained its humble character as pilgrims in monk's habit, many carrying crosses or walking bare-footed, make their way slowly through the town.

Procession of the Plague, Tournai (Doornik), second Sunday in

September. In 1092, Tournai was delivered from the Plague through the intercession of Notre Dame aux Malades. Today, the gratitude and homage of its citizens is symbolised by one of the richest and most colourful processions in the country. Divided into three sections, it honours the patron saints of all the parishes of the city, the statues of Our Lady, and concludes with the Bishop of Tournai and the Cathedral clergy, preceded by trumpeters and choir.

Candle Procession, Montaigu (Scherpenheuvel), first Sunday after All Saints Day. The most impressive of the many pilgrimages which take place from May to November to Our Lady of Montaigu. Pilgrims carrying thousands of candles walk round the church and cemetery while bells ring. The remains of these candles are said to be invested with the power to cure any number of ills—a power which continues for one year until the next Candle Procession takes place.

Nativity Plays, several towns and villages, prior to Christmas. Cribs are set up in all towns, but especially interesting are the living cribs of " Outre Meuse " arranged in the open air near the churches at Liège (Luik). At Liège, too, ancient puppets enact the Nativity Play, a most popular event. At Vosselaar, the inhabitants make up charming scenes to evoke the Birth of Christ. At Saint-Severin-en-Condroz, the villagers take part in excellent living tableaux.

SPORTING FIXTURES

International Rowing Competition, Bredene and Ostend, early June. Takes place on the Bruges Canal.

Grand Prix des Frontières, Chimay, early June. International motor and motor-cycle racing.

Grand Prix de Belgique, Francorchamps, about mid-June. The most important motor racing event of the year in Belgium.

Grand Prix de Belgique, Francorchamps, early July. The most important motor-cycle event of the year in Belgium.

International Steeplechase, Gaverbeek Racecourse, Waregem, last Tuesday of August.

Liège-Rome-Liège International Car Rally. Starting from Spa at the end of August, returning there early in September.

TRADE FAIRS

International Motor Show, Brussels, January.
International Spring Fair, Charleroi, end of March to early April.
International Brussels Fair, end of April to early May.
International Liège Fair, end of May to early June.
International Flanders Fair, Ghent, two weeks in September.

TRADITIONAL CUSTOMS

Kattestoet (Cat Procession), Ieper (Ypres), second Sunday in May. Two local giants accompany this famous procession, which evokes legends featuring these four-footed friends. In olden days, the Jester of Ypres then threw live cats from the top of the belfry on to the spectators below. Today, fortunately, he contents himself with showering velvet replicas instead !

Matrimonial Tea Party, Ecaussines-Lalaing, Whit Monday. This unusual annual gathering of bachelors and spinsters for an outdoor tea party and dancing has become a great draw both for the young people taking part and onlooking visitors. Participants (men must wear full bridegrooms' dress) wear a symbolic cup on their lapels and all are received with due ceremony by the burgomaster and town band. No statistics are available concerning the number of matches resulting from this event, but it is certainly an occasion for fun and good humour.

Procession of St. Guidon, Anderlecht, Whit Monday. An historical procession in honour of the local patron saint is accompanied by a fair, cattle market and assembly of decorated horses and carts.

March of St. Rolanda, Gerpinnes, Whit Monday. Old-time uniforms, martial music, pomp and ceremony provide the traditional military trimmings to this annual liturgical procession. · A similar tradition is embodied in the **March of St. Peter** at Florennes and the **March of our Lady** at Walcourt on Trinity Sunday.

Procession of the Golden Chariot, * Mons (Bergen), Trinity Sunday. Historical pageantry recalls the power, piety and wealth of the Noble Chapter of the Deaconesses of St. Waltrudis, and includes canonesses and craftsmen who might have stepped out of some Old Master. St. George appears leading the dreadful dragon Doudou, who is gloriously defeated later in the day. During a fierce battle, Doudou's terrible tail sweeps everything before it to the terror and joy of onlookers.

Grand Ommegang, * Brussels, takes place irregularly and usually in conjunction with some other outstanding event (e.g. the last occasion was during the Brussels Exhibition in 1958). It is a gay and glorious affair in which an historical procession is linked with tableaux embodying all the main themes of Belgian folklore. However, every year a smaller **Ommegang** is organised, usually at the opening of the Brussels *Kermesse* (Fair) on July 21st. No pageantry could have a better setting than Brussels' Grand'Place, one of the sightseeing gems of Europe, dominated by the beautifully proportioned Town Hall, which was begun in 1402.

Day of the Four Pageants, Tournai (Doornik), second Sunday in June. Artistry and folklore are the main features of the four great pageants that unfold through the town. The three themes of Porcelain, Flowers and Folklore are followed by a traditional Publicity Pageant.

Flying Cat Ceremony, Verviers, Sunday in June. Verviers concludes its great annual fancy-dress procession by launching a toy cat attached to a small balloon from the tower of the old church of St. Remacle. The tradition is said to be based on historic fact: in 1641, a Verviers apothecary made his own experiment in aerodynamics by launching a live cat attached to blown-up pigs' bladders from the same tower. The cat landed on its paws and ran away !

Shrimp Festival, Oostduinkerke, early July. This is the last of Belgium's many huge beaches where one can still see the picturesque custom of shrimping on horseback. Mounted shrimpers drag trawl nets through the water at low tide, and afterwards the freshly boiled shrimps are offered for sale.

Procession of the Golden Tree, Bruges, July, every five years. In 1486, the wedding of Charles the Bold to the English Princess Margaret of York was the most splendid feast this old Hanseatic town had ever seen. Named the Pageant of the Golden Tree after the symbol of the tournament held on this occasion by the Knights of the Golden Fleece, it has recently been revived as an historical procession of great beauty.

Hops Festival, Poperinghe, first Sunday in September. Festivities include a picturesque procession, a hop gathering competition on the market square, election of " Queen of the Hops," and, at night, the traditional burning of Hommelvent (Hop-man), symbolising the end of the harvest.

Brueghelian Festivities, Wingene, second Sunday in September. Inspired by the paintings of Peter Brueghel, Wingene relives his famous works and the colourful country roughness of its past with pageantry and a torchlight procession. In the evening, a thousand players in 16th century costume sit down to a Brueghelian meal of brown bread, sausages and rice pudding. Such Brueghelian characters can be seen, too, at some of the annual *Kermesses*, or fairs, in the country.

Oktober Feesten, Wieze, end of September to early October. Based on the traditional Beer Feasts of Munich, this is one of the most popular events of its kind in Belgium. Processions, music and fancy dress are included in the programme, but the gastronomic highlight is the huge feast of roast chicken grilled on spits, or sausages cooked on an open fire, when the vast hall, built for the occasion, often proves too small ! Beer, of course, is also much in evidence throughout the festivities.

WINE AND FOOD FESTIVALS

Feast of Wine and Grapes, Overijse (Overyse), end of August to early September. Two weeks of festivities and entertainment include the crowning of the Queen of Grapes during a folklore play, a pageant of " Grapes in History," exhibitions of grapes and other produce, and dancing. A similar event occurs at Hoeilaart at the end of the month.

CHAPTER FIVE

Cyprus

ISLAND OF SUNSHINE, WINE, ANCIENT CULTURES AND RUGGED beauty, it is less generally known that Cyprus also has an active Ski Club and fine ski-ing terrain in the high hill resorts from January to March ! Her main annual events, however, are more concerned with deep religious belief and the products of her soil.

Festival of Epiphany, all over the island, January 6th. The commemoration of the Baptism is considered, in the Orthodox world, to be as important as Christmas or Easter. On this day, every family goes to church, taking wax candles to immerse in the Holy Water and, afterwards, the priest leads a procession to the sea or, inland, to the village well, for the Blessing of the Waters. In Limassol, Larnaca and Kyrenia, the ancient ceremony of Diving for the Cross is also observed, attended by crowds of people along the waterfront and in rowing boats. After a procession from the church, a gold Cross is tied to a purple ribbon and, while prayers are intoned, it is lowered to the water and drawn up again. This is done twice. Then the ribbon is wrapped round the Cross and the priest flings it out into the sea. A number of men or boys plunge in after it, compet ng for the honour of returning it to the priest.

Limassol Carnival, Limassol, for a week ending on the Sunday before Ash Monday. Costumed processions, dancing, singing and general festivity are the main features of this gay carnival period. It reaches its climax on the second Sunday with a Grand Procession of masked figures and decorated chariots.

Flower Festivals (Anthestiria), in all main towns, May. Floral parades, usually held in the stadiums, include chariots depicting themes from ancient Greek mythology and present-day life in Cyprus. Afterwards, children from the secondary schools usually put on a colourful display of traditional Cypriot dances.

Cyprus Trade Fair, Nicosia, usually mid-June to mid-July. Participants mostly include neighbouring countries such as Greece, Turkey, Israel, Italy, etc.

Platres Festival, Platres, September 8th-11th. Main features of this festival, held in the picturesque mountain resort of Platres, are an agricultural show, a local arts and crafts display, folk dancing and singing performances.

CHAPTER SIX

Denmark

NOTHING JARS IN DENMARK. THE LAND IS GREEN AND PLEASANT and fertile; the beaches are as wide and smooth as any in Europe; the people are gay and open-hearted.

The Danish spirit is nowhere better reflected than in Copenhagen's Tivoli Gardens, whose programme of entertainments between May and September has become famous all over the world. Here you will find popular entertainment at its highest level, from funfair and light music to symphony concerts and ballet. Tivoli at night is fairylike, and on fête nights its firework displays are really exceptional.

As far as ballet is concerned, however, there is nothing in Denmark and little in the rest of Europe to compare with the Royal Danish Ballet and Music Festival in May, the leading cultural event on the Danish calendar. Amongst national rejoicings, Midsummer Eve on June 23rd is perhaps the greatest. In fact, visitors to Denmark in the early summer are especially well catered for.

AGRICULTURAL, HORTICULTURAL AND LIVESTOCK SHOWS

Bellahøj Livestock Show and Agricultural Fair, Copenhagen, last week-end of June or first week-end in July.

Ho Sheep Market, mid-way between Varde and Esbjerg, last week-end in August. The last of its kind. Between 1,000-1,500 sheep are driven in from the sand dunes of West Jutland to the tiny hamlet of Ho.

CULTURAL EVENTS

Royal Danish Ballet and Music Festival, Copenhagen, last two weeks of May. Music and drama enthusiasts heading for Scandinavia can enjoy a positive feast of festivals now that those of Copenhagen, Bergen, Stockholm and Helsinki have been arranged in conjunction with each other within a five-week period. The first of the four is at Copenhagen and includes performances by the famous Royal Danish Ballet, opera and concerts. During the Festival period, a concert of organ music by Buxtehude is played in the castle church at Frederiksborg on the famous Compenius Organ, built in 1634 and still in its original state. At Odense, there's a Carl Nielsen concert.

Fanø, Denmark   *Dancing on the Sands*

Salzburg, Austria   " *Everyman* "

Les Baux, France *Midnight Mass* Riquewihr, France *Wine Festi*

Ste. Anne-la-Palud, France " *Pardon* "

Hamlet Festival, Helsingør (Elsinore), second and third weeks in June at irregular intervals. Usually members of a famous foreign theatrical company are invited to enact Shakespeare's play in the court-yard of the castle which inspired it.

NATIONAL OR SPECIAL DAYS

H.M. Queen Ingrid's Birthday, March 28th, Copenhagen. Colourful military parade and concert in Amalienborg Square.

Tivoli Season, Copenhagen, May 1st to second Sunday in September. World famous—and justifiably so—for the variety of their entertainment, the Tivoli Gardens truly offer something for everyone in a setting which is really lovely, especially at night when they are spangled with thousands of coloured lights. Out of the tremendous range of entertainments, all of them excellent, I must mention specially the Pantomime and the Tivoli Guards. The former is unique of its kind, for here is the only place in the world where the old original Italian pantomimes with Pantaloon, Columbine and Harlequin are shown regularly, with all the original *pas* and burlesques, and with the original musical scores. The Tivoli Guards, dressed in similar uniforms to those worn by the Royal Guard, are made up entirely of youngsters, and the band is especially delightful, its small drummers hardly bigger than the drums they handle so effectively. Entrance to Tivoli Gardens costs very little, but most of the special shows ask additional fees, usually at a most reasonable level so that you can enjoy yourself on a very limited budget.

National Flag Day, all over the country, June 15th. A public holiday in honour of the oldest flag in the world.

Midsummer Eve, all over the country, June 23rd. Every Dane takes part in this national rejoicing for the longest day of the year. Along the coast, particularly north of Copenhagen, thousands of bonfires fling their sparks into the long twilight. A " witch " is burned, too, in some places, a reminder of one of the less happy customs of the 17th century—though, of course, in the 20th century version the lady is not alive !

American Independence Day, Rebild (Danish-American National Park), July 4th. Perhaps the biggest event of its kind outside the United States is attended by a combined American-Danish gathering of about 40,000. It includes musical and vocal entertainment and an exchange of greetings by leading spokesmen from the two nations.

Look Around Day, Copenhagen, late August or early September. Catering for the curious, the Copenhagen Journalists' Union have arranged this day when a large number of institutions open doors normally closed to the public. Admission tickets are also lottery tickets, with the possibility of winning any one of a large number of prizes. There is a special Tivoli festival night. Note, though, that tickets sell out well in advance.

C

SPORTING FIXTURES

The Danish Derby, Klampenborg Race Course, Copenhagen, during second half of June. Biggest race of the year in Denmark.

International Sound Regatta, off Copenhagen, July. Open to all classes of yacht.

International Sea Fishing Festival, Mommark, late August or early September. Teams from many countries take part in this four-day event, which includes prizes for the biggest and heaviest catches of different types of fish. On the last day, competitors' wives can go along and watch husbands at sea.

TRADE FAIRS

Danish Food Fair, Aalborg, in June in years with uneven numbers.

Danish Industries Fair, Fredericia, early August. Largest of its kind in Denmark.

Scandinavian Design Cavalcade, Copenhagen, from early September. Exhibitions and window displays all over the city put Danish arts, crafts and industrial design on show. A similar cavalcade takes place simultaneously in Oslo, Stockholm and Helsinki.

TRADITIONAL CUSTOMS

Traditional Students' Celebration, Copenhagen, end of June. Giving vent to their high spirits after graduation, Copenhagen students converge on the Equestrian Statue outside the Royal Theatre and dance around it. Students in midwifery have taken up the tradition, too, and after their graduation join hands to dance joyously—and most appropriately!—round the Storks' Fountain at the Amagertorv in the city centre.

Viking Festival, Frederikssund, late June or early July. Beards become two a penny amongst the citizens of Frederikssund, who grow them specially for the two weeks of colourful pageantry. This annual revival of ancient Danish history takes the form of one of several Viking plays.

Tilting Tournament, Sønderborg, second or third week-end in July. Armoured knights used to do this for fun, and so, today, do horsemen in south Jutland and other parts of Denmark. The main event takes place in an open stadium at Sønderborg when galloping horsemen with lances must remove a small ring dangling from a gallows. The ring becomes progressively smaller as riders are eliminated, until the winner and runner-up have been established Tilting King and Crown Prince of the year.

Sønderho Days, south Fanø, third week-end in July. During a civic festival in this old seafaring centre, all the inhabitants wear traditional costume and there's a display of old fishermen's dances on the sands.

Fanø, in fact, is about the only part of Denmark where traditional costumes may sometimes be seen in everyday use.

Children's " Shooting the Parrot," Skelskør, week-end in late July. This is a weekend for the youngsters, who form their own pageant and, on the second day, march to the nearby forest where the shooting takes place. Golden apples dangle from a parrot perched on top of a high pole, and must be shot down with ancient rifles in the correct sequence. The winner is proclaimed King of Birds.

CHAPTER SEVEN

Finland

HARD WINTERS, SHORT BRILLIANT SUMMERS AND THE FINNS'
own love for their wild spacious countryside have moulded their national
character and are reflected in both their popular and cultural festivities.
July and August may be the hottest months, but June days are warm,
too, and include Finland's two greatest annual events: the national
rejoicings at Midsummer and the Sibelius Festival whose music draws
so much of its inspiration from the moods of Finnish nature.

CULTURAL EVENTS

Sibelius Festival, Helsinki, June. In his music, Sibelius has captured
all the wildness and the gentleness of his native countryside. Much of
his work, too, was inspired by the granite valour of legendary heroes as
recorded in Finland's great epic poem, *Kalevala*. It has earned him
admiration abroad, reverence in his own land, and this musical week
is almost entirely devoted to his work. Most of the concerts are held at
Helsinki University bordering the Senate Square. Dominated by the
green domes of the Cathedral, the proportions and classical lines of this
Square make it, in my opinion, the finest in Scandinavia.

Turku Music Festival, Turku, a week in June. Classical music
in the romantic setting of Turku's medieval cathedral and castle.

Outdoor Drama Festival, Nurmijärvi, July. An annual tribute
to Aleksis Kivi who, in the last century, was the first novelist and play-
wright to write in the Finnish language and remains the best known
Finnish classical writer outside Finland.

St. Olaf Festival, Savonlinna, August. Music festival with folk
dancing and outdoor drama performances in the courtyard of Savonlinna's 15th century castle.

NATIONAL OR SPECIAL DAYS

Vappu (May Day), all over the country, May 1st. Originally a
festival to celebrate the return of spring after the long northern winter,
May 1st has also since been adopted as Labour Day. The students have
adopted it, too, and at midnight on *vapunaatto* (May Day Eve) everyone
who is or ever has been a student dons their student cap, while an
intrepid one wades through a fountain to place a cap on the head of the

Havis Amanda statue near the South Harbour. Balloons and *vappu* fans are on sale everywhere; hotels run special dances, and it's a grand excuse for all-night revelry. On May Day itself students form a procession through the streets of Helsinki, culminating in big open air gatherings and choral concerts. Workers in most provincial towns and villages have their processions, too.

Juhannus (**Midsummer Day**), all over the country, the nearest Saturday to June 24th. Few people, including the youngsters, get to bed on *Juhannusaatto* (Midsummer Eve) which celebrates the longest day of the year. On lake shores up and down the country bonfires flicker in the twilight of the brief northern night, while north of the Arctic Circle the sun works tirelessly round the clock. Special late performances are held at open air theatres in most towns, and dances are arranged at all hotels.

Independence Day, all over the country, December 6th. A public holiday, with military parades in Helsinki and Gala Performances at the National Theatre.

RELIGIOUS EVENTS

Lapp Church Festivals, Finnish Lapland, held at main villages such as Inari and Enontekiö on Lady Day (a Sunday in March), at Easter and early in September. On these occasions, Lapps in their brilliant costumes come in from their remote homesteads to take part in a special church service, usually followed by a programme of festivities. The Lady Day festival continues with lasso-throwing contests and ski-joring races with reindeer on the frozen lake. Colourful Lapp weddings are often arranged to take place during these Festivals.

SPORTING FIXTURES

Salpausselkä International Winter Games, Lahti, March. Two-day competitions including cross-country racing, ski jumping, downhill and slalom races.

Ounasvaara International Winter Games, Rovaniemi, end of March. Ski-ing competitions on the Arctic Circle.

Log Rolling Contests, various parts of the country, June or July. Skilful loggers, with an amazing sense of balance, travel downstream through rapids precariously perched on a log.

TRADE FAIRS

Scandinavian Design Cavalcade, Helsinki, September. Finnish arts, crafts and industrial design on show in shops and exhibitions.

TRADITIONAL CUSTOMS

Reindeer Round-ups, Finnish Lapland, December to March. Scattered herds are rounded up in corrals all over Finnish Lapland for sorting, counting, slaughter and marking by their owners in a scene that resembles a wild west film in Arctic surroundings.   Round-ups usually last for one to three days, and I have fond memories of one night shared with two Finns and a dozen Lapps in a log hut the size of a postage stamp ! The more accessible corrals are to be found near Ivalo on the Arctic Highway, four hours by air from Helsinki.

CHAPTER EIGHT

France

THERE IS NO EUROPEAN COUNTRY WHICH IS SO LITTLE-KNOWN
as France. The vast majority of tourists seem content to visit Paris, the
French Riviera and, to a lesser extent, Brittany. Yet, this loveliest of
lands has many other fascinating and richly rewarding districts. Exploring
this other France can bring you to enchanting spots.

There is a rich variety of festivals, too, which offer ideas for holidays
with a purpose. In the shadow of palace or castle wall, in an ancient
square or in a garden, the trestles go up and in the stillness of the night
music and drama take on a new quality. These unusual settings do, in
fact, allow us to escape from the traditional restrictions of hall and
theatre, and open to the creative producer new possibilities of experi-
menting with novel conceptions. Many old masterpieces also have been
brought a new life at these festivals.

This chapter will, I hope, indicate that every type of festival is to be
found in France, from the riotous carnival at Nice to the more serious
pilgrimages to Lourdes. Make up your mind, therefore, to choose your
own reward—a reward which is available throughout the year, but more
especially in the summer months.

AGRICULTURAL, HORTICULTURAL AND LIVESTOCK
SHOWS

The outstanding **agricultural show** is that staged by the Salon
Général de l'Agriculture, and it is usually held in Paris. Of historic
interest is the **Horse Fair** held at Lessay (Normandy) in June; it
originated in the 14th century.

Of all the Spring flower fêtes there is none more colourful than the
Jonquil Festival at Gerardmer. This resort in the Vosges mountains
is on the edge of a fine lake and amidst spectacular fir forests. In April,
after the melting of the snows on the mountains, the slopes are carpeted
with wild flowers, and principally with jonquils, the rush-leaved daffodil
of the most delicate tone of yellow. For the festival (April 23rd), the
whole town is covered with myriads of these flowers, and the fête itself
is a form of rejoicing, as the jonquil is the sure sign that Winter is over
and Spring has come, and the gaiety of the festival is natural and spon-
taneous.

33

Along the resorts of the French Riviera, and notably at Menton, there are **floral displays** on frequent occasions, while the Flower Markets are always a source of colourful delight.

CARNIVALS

Carnival festivities are a survival of ancient ceremonies welcoming the return of spring. The traditions of these festivals are still preserved in many towns of France. The most important event is, undoubtedly:

Nice Carnival, for 12 days prior to Shrove Tuesday. These world famous festivities are spread over a distance of a mile and a half: processions of decorated floats, flowered corsos, cavalcades, battles of confetti, battles of flowers, follow one upon the other during 12 days. On the last day (Shrove Tuesday) there is a stupendous firework display, lighting up the entire Bay of Angels, during which the King Carnival is burnt. The organisation of this carnival takes up months in preparations, while the construction of the " Giants " has been the speciality of a few families of artisans who hand down their art from father to son.

Other notable carnival fêtes are held at **Amelie-les-Bains, Albi, Chalon-sur-Saone, Dunkirk** and **Granville.**

Apart from the pre-Lenten carnivals, there are also similar events taking place during the summer and autumn. At **Annemasse** (Savoy) there is a carnival cavalcade early in October; at **Douai,** the Festival of the Giants, the Sunday following July 5th and the two following days. During these three days and nights the giant, Gayant, is taken in procession through the streets while the drums beat and the church bells sound. Gayant is about 25 feet high, is clad in military uniform, and is followed by Marie Gagenon, who is Madame Gayant and about 20 feet high, and is always dressed in the latest fashion. There are three children, Jacquot, Fillion and the squinting baby, Binbin. The giants leave their home (2 Rue de Lambres) and go to the Town Hall to salute the mayor, after which they proceed to the Place d'Armes and take part in the carnival festivities.

On Whit Monday the traditional procession of the giants of France and Belgium takes place in Lille, in the course of which more than 100 of these fabulous creatures, from 12 to 18 feet high and weighing up to 15 cwts. each, are taken in procession through the principal streets of the town. These traditional giants are relics of the Spanish domination of the Netherlands and used to be wickerwork supported by a light wooden frame. Nowadays they are often made in plastic materials. Towns who send their giants to Lille include Bailleul, Cambrai, Valenciennes, Hazebrouck, Denain and Dunkirk.

Remiremont (Vosges) holds its summer carnival at the end of July.

Sainte-Marie-aux-Mines, mid-June. A peasants' carnival with floats illustrating the life and customs of the local people. Masked balls are held at night in all the surrounding towns and villages.

Saint-Quentin, Whit-Sunday. After a street procession a folklore festival is held in front of the municipal theatre.

Tours, end of May. Carnival festivities, with a central theme.

CULTURAL EVENTS

There are many music and drama festivals in France. Among the outstanding music festivals are those at:

Bordeaux, end of May. In this important French seaport and the town of fine wines, the climate is particularly pleasant at the time of this festival and lends great charm to chamber-concerts given in historic places such as the Château de la Brède or the Château d'Yquem. Its theatre is one of the most beautiful in France.

Strasbourg, early or mid-June. Standing at the cross-roads of French and German culture, this city is a centre where men and movements come together. It has a superb tradition of performances of the great religious works in its magnificent Cathedral, and a walk in the picturesque old Alsatian streets is a restful and enjoyable prelude.

Aix-en-Provence, mid- to end of July. Here you find established a tradition in the interpretation of Mozart. In the delightful auditorium of the Archbishop's Palace, Mozart operas as well as other classical or contemporary works are produced with exquisite taste, creations of international co-operation stimulated by the lightness and purity of the Mediterranean air. Aix-en-Provence is also one of the most delightful—perhaps the *most* delightful—of French provincial cities.

Besançon, September. This city reveals charming architecture of distant Spanish origin that offers delightful surprises at every turn. The restful landscape of provincial France gives a delicious feeling of relaxation as one listens to chamber music or sacred music or to concerts by the finest French orchestras with famous conductors and soloists. Then there is the infectious enthusiasm of young people who have come from all over the world for the annual competition for young conductors.

Prades, July. In this small town in the Pyrenees Bach concerts arranged by Pablo Casals, the great 'cellist, are an important musical occasion.

Other pleasant but less important music festivals in France include:
Dieppe, Chamber Music Concerts, August.
Menton, Music Festival, early August.
Mulhouse, Symphonic and Chamber Music, June-August.
Nantes, Musical Month, May.
Sceaux, Nights of Sceaux (Concerts of French Music), May and June.
Toulouse, International Singing Competition, early October.
Versailles, Musical May, early May.

Aix-les-Bains, International Dance Festival, end of July.
Divonne-les-Bains, International Chamber Music Festival, July.
Royaumont, Concerts in the setting of the Cistercian Abbey, June.
Among the dramatic and ballet festivals, the following should be noted:
Nîmes, plays, June.
Avignon, Festival of Dramatic Art, end of July.
Amiens, plays, late May.
Arles, Festival in Roman Theatre, end of June.
La Baule, theatrical performances, during summer.
Blois, dramatic art, early July.
Orange, drama, music, dancing in ancient theatre, end of July.
Poitiers, Festival of Dramatic Art, early May.
St. Malo, Dramatic Art Performance, mid-July.

The Festival of the Burgund an Nights takes place all through Burgundy from June to mid-August and covers many art forms. D jon is one of the main centres, with performances in the National Theatre and the Ducal Palace, while there are religious concerts in the Cathedral. The church of Saint Pierre in Macon, the noble cathedral of Sens and the cathedral at Auxerre also provide superb backgrounds for concerts and drama. Beaune plays its part in this fest val, and there are various performances at the Abbey of Brou, Beaune, Gray, Alésia, Pontarlier, Bussy-Rabutin and Salins-les-Bains—often in historic surroundings. A programme of events can be obtained from the Tourist Office, D jon.

The **Film Fest val** held each year in April and May at Cannes has international renown, and most countries send in entries, while many famous stars (and starlets) are to be seen. Smaller film festivals include a telev sion-film one at Monte Carlo.

" **Sound and Light** " performances began in the Loire valley and those in the grounds of the delightful chateaux are still the most popular. Many other outstanding French historical buildings have followed their lead. In addition, many other buildings are floodlit through the summer and present spectacles of considerable beauty. A list of the " Sound and Light " performances is given in the " Calendar of Events," available from the French Government Tourist Office. Three I would specially recommend are: Versailles, Chambord and Chenonceaux.

NATIONAL OR SPECIAL DAYS

Easily the outstanding French national celebration is " **Quatorze Juillet** " (July 14th) which is the anniversary of the fall of the Bastille. I must warn you it is a very noisy affair, and also that for two days after it most shops are closed and most public services disorganised. Perhaps the best place to witness the scene is in Paris, *although there are celebrations in every city, town, and village.* The French have a passion for fairs—it must be a major industry, in fact—so if you go to Montmartre you will find in the streets merry-go-rounds, stalls, booths, shooting galleries, and all the fun of the fair. At one time the music (!) provided by the competing attractions was deafening, and anyone living in the neighbourhood must have had very little sleep; but nowadays some law seems to have been passed forbidding these steam-organs, which in a way rather detracts from the jollity, but is otherwise merciful. This does not stop, of course, pavement music, with crowds of people dancing everywhere in the streets. Officially, there is a military parade down the Champs-Elysées on the morning of July 14th, attended by the President, which draws great crowds. The phlegmatic Anglo-Saxon must expect to be kissed by strangers, pondering perhaps on the French genius for mass disturbance. *Mi- Carême*, which takes place in mid-Lent, is the most important fête after *Quatorze Juillet*. Again on this day excited folk, many in fancy dress, are everywhere, and in the afternoon the queens of all the *arrondissements* (districts), chosen by popular vote during preceding weeks, are paraded through the streets in decorated cars. There are several other entertaining fairs held in Paris, and information regarding the dates can be obtained from the Information Offices, to be found in all the railway stations and elsewhere.

November 11th (**Armistice Day**) is another important event in France, and attracts much more attention than it does in Britain. There are processions and speeches, but despite all this show of patriotism I have found that many of the war memorials erected after the First World War are in a sorry and neglected state; and many of them are frankly hideous.

Joan of Arc Festivals are held in Orleans, Rouen and Domremy (her birthplace) around May 8th.

RELIGIOUS FESTIVALS

France was one of the first countries to embrace the Christian faith. The veneration paid to saints and their relics promoted the establishment of many religious centres, including great abbeys. Every year great flocks of pilgrims still travel to famous shrines: Lourdes, Lisieux, Fourvières and Paray-le-Monial. Many local celebrations have lost nothing of their spiritual and picturesque appeal: the " Pardons " in Brittany and the festival of the Saintes-Maries-de-la-Mer are especially notable.

A country of freedom and tolerance, France offers places of worship for persons of practically every faith. In this section I list some of the more outstanding religious festivals.

Fête of Saint Vincent, Burgundy, end of January. This festival is celebrated one year in a Côte de Nuits village and the next in a Côte de Beaune village. All the statues of the saint, brought from each village of the Côte, make a picturesque procession through the decorated streets, escorted by vineyard workers, Chevaliers du Tastevin in their rich costumes, and the banners of many confraternities.   There is a Solemn Mass and Banquet.

Anniversary of the First Appearance of the Virgin to Bernadette, Lourdes, February 11th.

Pilgrimage to Jouarre Abbey, traditional Mass since the ninth century, May 22nd.

Festival of St. Erasmus (Patron Saint of fishermen), Ajaccio (Corsica), June 2nd. Procession and blessing of the boats in the ports.

Corpus Christi, Basque folklore processions at Itxassou, Bidarray, Mendionde, Saint-Etienne-de-Baigorry; also in Finistère.

Festival of St. John the Baptist, Barbentane, end of June. Religious and secular celebrations.

Blessing of the Mules, Amélie-les-Bains, end of June. Takes place on the Feast of St. John (St. John's Day Fires). A similar celebration is to be seen at Arles-sur-Tech, both places being in the Pyrenees. Also held at Amélie is an **international folklore festival** in September.

" Charités " of Saint Martin, Tours, early July. Ceremonies at the Cathedral, the Basilica and Marmoutiers.

Fête of Saint Fleuret, Estaing, Aveyron, early July. For hours the procession of the Holy Body winds its way through the streets of this medieval town, situated in one of the most attractive parts of the Rouergue.

Festival of Saint Abdon and Saint Sennen, Arles-sur-Tech, end of July. The relics of the two saints and the " Rodella " of Montbolla are carried in procession.

Votive Feast of the Madeleine, Château-Renard-de-Provence, early August. Procession with the traditional farm-cart carrying the products of the soil.

Grand Procession of Our Lady, Le Puy, mid-August. Our Lady of Le Puy was one of the most celebrated places of pilgrimage in the Middle Ages.

Festival of the Mountains, Le Vigan, end of July. A notable religious event held on the summit of the Aîgoual, followed by regional and folklore festivities in the forests.

Assembly at **" Desert Museum,"** Anduze-Mas-Soubeyran, early September. This commemorates the martyrs of the " Desert," the Huguenot bush-land where, for a quarter of a century, bitter struggles provoked by the Edict of Nantes in 1685 were waged.

CHRISTMAS

The birth of Christ is celebrated throughout France on the night of Christmas Eve and the morning of Christmas Day. After the Midnight

Mass it is traditional to "réveilloner," to enjoy Christmas fare in the course of a very late supper in an atmosphere of unstudied gaiety. In some villages the celebration of this feast takes the form of a revival of very ancient religious traditions, in particular at Les Baux. To the beating of tambourines, shepherds and shepherdesses carrying each a candle enter the small church. Two shepherds offer up a lamb with prayers. The shepherdesses bear gifts for the Child. A splendidly combed and decorated ram draws a little painted chariot bearing the lamb, perfumed and ornamented. The first shepherd offers the lamb, then passes it to the shepherdess alongside him to offer in her turn, and thus from shepherd to shepherdess until all have made their offering. This annual ceremony is attended by great crowds of visitors motoring up from Marseilles and elsewhere. There is no hotel accommodation in Les Baux itself—it is a "dead town." So, anyone wishing to be present would have to arrange to stay at either St. Remy, Arles, Avignon or even Marseilles. (I should add there is actually a luxury, three-starred hotel on the outskirts of Les Baux, but it has only 10 bedrooms.)

A rather similar kind of Midnight Mass is held at **Saint-Paul-de-Vence** (outside of Nice), while other occasions of this kind to be specially noted are:

Brancion, Vineyard Workers' Midnight Mass.

Châteauneuf, Midnight Mass and Medieval Christmas Dinner in the Guard Room of the Castle.

Dourgnes, Midnight Mass at Saint-Benoit d'Encalcart.

Montpelier, Midnight Mass at the Enclos Chapel.

Perouges, a torchlight procession through the streets of this perfectly preserved walled medieval town (a National Monument) is followed by Midnight Mass in the fortress church, and then a gargantuan and gastronomic Réveillon supper which lasts over three hours; it is held in the ancient Hostellerie Vieux Pérouges—a museum in itself.

Saint-Benoit-sur-Loire, Midnight Mass at the Abbey church.

Paris, Midnight Mass at St. Eustache, famous for its singing; tickets are required—write to M. Le Curé enclosing an International Reply Coupon.

Solesmes* (south-west of Le Mans, with Sable-sur-Sarthe the nearest railway station). The Abbey Church is famous for its Gregorian Chant which is sung at Midnight Mass—an unforgettable experience.

HOLY WEEK

Holy Week is solemnly celebrated throughout France. The ancient traditions of processions and of Mysteries still live and give rise to moving ceremonies. Among the most notable are:

Arles-sur-Tech, Night-time procession of Black Penitents, Maundy Thursday.

Saugues, Penitential Procession (originated in the 12th century), Maundy Thursday.

Bonifacio, Calvi and **Sartène,** Corsica: Good Friday processions by night, in which hooded confraternities take part. The Sarténe procession, the " Catenacciu," is the most impressive. A hooded " Christ Enchained " is carried through the town. He, whose identity is never known, is chosen amongst the many who apply and who hope, if they are accepted, to earn remission of their sins thereby. The procession enacts Christ's climb up to Calvary.

At **Perpignan,** the " Sanch " is a moving procession, which first took place in 1416. Following a huge black and gold cross and the statues of Saint Veronica, " Mater Dolorosa " and " Ecce Homo," the hooded penitents enact, for the crowds massed in the narrow streets, the drama of Calvary.

Among the Easter ceremonies, particularly impressive ones are held at **Lourdes, Solesmes,** and **Saint-Benoit-sur-Loire.**

PILGRIMAGES

To visit the principal sanctuaries and take part in the most important religious events, the pilgrim as well as the holidaymaker who comes to France has the choice of several itineraries running through the best-known parts of the country. Starting from Paris the route could be to **Chartres** (where in mid-May there is the Pilgrimage of Students, who make the journey on foot from Paris); **Lisieux** (the home of Ste-Thérése de l'Enfant Jésus, the main pilgrimages being on August 15th and September 30th), **Mont Saint-Michel** (" La Merveille "); thence on to **Lourdes,** following possibly the road of the pilgrims of Saint James of Compostela, which in the Middle Ages was one of the outstanding religious journeys to be made in Europe. Second only to Rome, Lourdes is the most venerated of holy places in the Catholic world. To this small and lovely town in the Pyrenees about 600,000 pilgrims come annually, to see the miraculous Grotto of Massabielle, where in 1858 Bernadette Soubirous declared that the Virgin had appeared to her several times. The most important celebrations take place on August 15th, but all through the summer the town is a pilgrimage goal.

Paray-le-Mondial is, next to Lourdes and Lisieux, the most important French pilgrimage centre. It is the cradle of the devotion to the Sacred Heart of Jesus, a devotion which is world-wide. Pilgrims flock here in great numbers, especially on October 17th, the feast of Saint Margaret Mary, a humble nun to whom Christ revealed himself in 1673.

Roc-Amadour. In this tiny village, on a nearby high rock, there nestles the sanctuary which attracts many pilgrims between September

8th to 15th. This village was one of the stages on the road to Saint James of Compostela. Roland is said to have come here, and Saint Louis, and Louis XI. The pilgrims climb the rock stairs on their knees to reach the sanctuary and venerate the Black Virgin (a sixth century wooden statue). The site is one of the loveliest in France.

Ronchamp, September 8th. A pilgrimage to the modern chapel designed by Le Corbusier, Notre-Dame-du-Haut.

Les-Saintes-Maries-de-la-Mer, Gipsy Pilgrimage, May 24th-25th. The gipsies arrive from all parts of Europe to honour St. Sarah, their patron saint. According to the legend she landed here, after the Crucifixion, with Saint Mary Jacobeus, Saint Mary Salome, and some others. The statues of the Saints are carried in procession to the seashore, with an escort of " gardians," the mounted cowboys of the Camargue, in the midst of a most picturesque crowd. The bearers of the " boat " go into the sea for the rite of the aspersion of the Saints. For the return, the gipsies don white tunics and are granted the privilege of carrying the " boat." For two days there are festivities. At the end of October there are again traditional religious festivals in this seaside town when the relics are taken down to the sea as in May, but this time there are only people of Provence present, and not the gipsies as in the Spring fête.

THE BRETON PARDONS

Perhaps the most distinctive of the religious observances in France are the Pardons which take place each year in Brittany. They take place in the churches, sometimes consecrated by the tradition of a thousand years. But although primarily of a religious nature these celebrations have now become less fervent and the secular, festival side has become too prominent, rather spoiling the mystic atmosphere of olden times. At the same time, these occasions offer an opportunity of having a sight of the old costumes, especially those worn by the women, and including a fine display of *coiffes* or head-dresses.

Pardons start with a religious procession, after which the lay festival commences. Modern dances, bagpipes, and the traditional Breton wrestling are among the possible attractions. The principal Pardons are:

Tréguier, Pardon of St. Yves, the patron saint of lawyers throughout the world, May 19th.

Rumengol, Grand Pardon,* Trinity Sunday.

Quimperlé, Pardon of the Birds, end of May. This delightful " pardon " is of no religious significance, but draws white-coiffed women and sailors of the French Navy to the edge of the Carnoët Forest where all sorts of little artificial birds are sold, and there are picnics, dancing and singing.

Saint-Brieuc, Pardon with torchlight procession, May 31st.

Douarnenez, Blessing of the Sea, second or third Sunday in June.

St. Tugen, Pardon, last Sunday but one in June.

Plouguerneau, Pardon of Saint-Michael, fifth Sunday after Whitsun.

Saint-Jean-du-Doigt, Pardon of Fire, June 23rd-24th.

Guingamp, Pardon of Our Lady of Succour, eve of first Sunday in July.

La Pointe du Raz, Pardon of Notre Dame des Naufrages, Sunday after July 3rd.

Sainte-Anne-d'Auray, Pardon de la Troménie,* July 25th-26th. This is the most popular Pardon in Brittany. There is a torchlight procession on the 25th, with floodlighting of the Basilica and a watch service. On the 26th, the Mass is celebrated with all doors open, and there is a solemn procession.

Roscoff, Pardon of Sainte-Barbe, third Sunday in July.

Concarneau, Festival of the Blue Fishing Nets, last Sunday but one in August.

Saint-Anne-la-Palud, Grand Pardon,* last Sunday in August.

Le Folgoet, Grand Pardon of Notre Dame,* late August or early September.

Carnac, Pardon des Chevaux à Saint-Eloy, second Sunday in September.

Pont-Aven, Pardon, third Sunday in September.

SPORTING FIXTURES

Almost every kind of sporting event is to be found in France. Perhaps the outstanding occasion each year is the **Tour de France,** a cycle race that takes the competitors through many parts of the countryside, where the roads along which the international competitors are to pass are lined with enthusiastic fans. The race covers three thousand miles and it lasts almost four weeks, the winner being acclaimed a national hero. Two other important cycling contests are a **six-day race** in Paris (March), and the **Championship of France** (June), near Paris.

The greatest of French motor-car races and one of the most important in Europe is the **24-hour Motor Race** at Le Mans (end of June). Other outstanding motor-racing events are the **12-hour Grand Prix** at Rheims (July), the **Grand Prix d'Albigeois** at Albi (end of May), **French Grand Prix** at Montlhéry (July), at Nîmes (late March), Marseilles (end April), Bordeaux (early May), Orleans (late May), and Rouen (end June).

International Tennis Championships are held in Paris (April), and important championships take place also at Nice, Cannes and Menton.

The French **Football Cup Final** takes place at the end of May in Colombes (Paris). Outstanding centres for **winter sports events** are Chamonix, Mégève, and Val d'Isère. While, in peaceful contrast, there is the **European salmon-fishing championship,** held at Navarrenx, in the Pyrenees, during April. Then, the spectacle of **bullfights** in the

, Belgium   *The Gilles*   Helsinki, Finland   *May Day*

Rothenburg, Germany   *Meistertrunk Play*

Hamelin, Germany   *The Pied Piper*

Landshut, Germany   *The Princely Wedding*

Spanish style is staged at Nîmes, Arles and Beziers during the summer months, on occasion.

There is **horse-racing** throughout France, Sunday being the favourite day. Near Paris, at Auteuil, there are some valuable races run; while Longchamp and especially Chantilly are both notable. Apart from the actual racing the main occasions are outstanding for their wonderful displays of ladies' fashions. There is also considerable elegance to be seen at Deauville during August, where the **Polo World Championship** is also played.

TRADE FAIRS

The outstanding general fairs of international standing are:

Lyons, early March.

Paris, mid- to end of May.

Strasbourg, early September.

There are many other specialised fairs, however, most of them staged in Paris. The Association Française des Salons Specialisés (22, Avenue Franklin-Roosevelt, Paris 8) can supply full details. Here I will only list a few of the most important shows:

International Air Show at Le Bourget airport, Paris (May).

International Boat Show, Cannes (August).

International Leather Week, Paris (September).

International Watch and Clock Show, Besançon (September).

National Radio and Television Show, Paris (September).

International Motor Show, Paris (October).

Note: Check exact dates, for they change from year to year.

TRADITIONAL CUSTOMS

Menton, Lemon Festival, during February. A picturesque fête for the lemon harvest, particularly abundant around Menton. This golden fruit is itself the principal item in the decoration of the streets. There is also an exhibition of useful and exotic plants.

Cannes, Mimosa Festival, during February.

Arles-sur-Tech, Festival of the Bear, mid-February.

Cap d'Antibes, Fête of the pinks, and displays of hydrangeas, early April.

Biarritz, Cannes, Deauville, Trouville, Easter Fêtes and Galas.

Gérardmer, Jonquil Festival, end of April.

Nice, Festival of the May Queens, during May. The squares are decorated with branches and flowers and the young people celebrate May. There is dancing every evening for the " re-birth."

Menton, May Festival.

Orleans, Joan of Arc Festival, early May.

Saint-Tropez, The Bravade, May 16th-18th. This curious ceremony

D

commemorates a rather unusual event, when in the 17th century an invasion by the Spaniards was threatened; but they were frightened away by a noisy demonstration. The help of St. Tropez, the martyr of Pisa, was invoked, of course, and his statue is carried through the street while blunderbusses are fired. Incidentally, there were no casualties on either side during this historic " battle." The following day there is a re-enactment of the proceedings, along with general rejoicings.

Biarritz, Cannes, Deauville, Trouville, Saint-Rémy-de-Provence, Festivals and galas, end of May.

Wissembourg, Traditional festival with folklore events, end of May.

Sceaux, Festival of the Nights of Sceaux, at the Pavillon de l'Aurore, in the Orangerie and the Park of the Little Château, May and June.

Aix-en Provence, Spring Festival, second fortnight in June.

Fête of Jeanne Hachette, Beauvais, June 28th. Jeanne Laisné (as she was born) helped in the defence of Beauvais when the town was besieged in 1472 by Charles the Bold, whose standard she brought down with a blow from her " hachette."

Sète, Fishermen's Fête, with water jousting, mid-June.

Saint-Jean-de-Luz, Saint John's Day Folklore Festival, end of June.

Tarascon, first of the " Tarasque " Fêtes, end of June. Legend tells of a monster hidden in the banks of the Rhône, capsizing ships, drowning the boatmen and devouring cattle and men. Sixteen valiant warriors went to fight the beast: eight of them were killed. Martha, the sister of Lazarus, is also said to have subdued the amphibious beast. At the first fête the Tarasque monster terrifies the population. Its body, in the shape of a huge egg, is covered with scales, between which long barbs of iron stick out. The eight knights the monster has devoured are now in its belly and work the furious Tarasque. It is a noisy occasion. The animal prances and rushes through the streets at full speed, throwing over people and belching smoke and fire out of its hideous jaws. Later, the farandole is danced in the town. On Ste. Martha's Day (in July), the second fête is a much more peaceful affair, and the Tarasque, who has now been suddenly tamed by the Saint, is led through the town at the end of a ribbon held by a young girl.

Palavas, Fishermen's Fête and Blessing of the sea. Water jousting in the Grand Canal, end of June. As in Sète and other ports in this part of France, water jousting is a popular sport. Each of the opposing boats is manned by a crew of ten oarsmen and six balancers, assisted by two musicians on the prow. The balancers sit on a sloping platform, swinging their legs above the water. The musicians play a small drum and a shrill *hautbois*, instruments as medieval as the sport itself. On a grandstand beside the canal sit the jury, who award points for each round. They are dressed, like the jousting teams, in immaculate white. The signal is given, and the boats sail toward each other, but it is not until the second passing that the attack is made. The jouster in each boat must try and push his opponent into the water. Victims are replaced by team mates, but a victor remains to fight again and possibly again until they, too, are vanquished. It's all grand fun.

Château-Renard-de-Provence, Feast of St. Eloi with traditional procession of the floats, early July.

Saint-Jean-de-Luz, International Folklore Festival, end of July.

Grasse, Jasmine Fête, end of July.

Vittel, Arcachon, Biarritz, Cannes, Deauville, Dinard, and most seaside resorts and spas, fêtes and galas, July and August.

Annecy, Festival on the Lake, early August.

Ajaccio, Commemorative Events on the occasion of Napoleon's birthday, August 15th.

Hendaye, Traditional Basque fête, mid-August.

Chamonix, Guides' Festival, mid-August.

Biarritz and Bayonne, Basque festivals, August.

Nancy, International Folklore Festival of the Mirabelle plum, end of August.

Dijon, Autumn Games and annual Fête of the Vines, early September. International Festival of Song and Dance. Folklore events. Dancing round the Barenzai fountain in which the new wine flows.

Ribeauvillé, Day of the Strolling Fiddlers, first Sunday in September. This is a typical Alsatian festival, and its origin is very ancient. Strolling musicians of the region came together in the past in the town to give homage to their suzerain, the lord of Ribeaupierre. The proceedings are very gay, there is a folklore procession, and there are free drinks at the Fountain of the Wine, the Town Hall Square.

Casamaccioli (Corsica), " Santa du Nioli," early September. Traditional procession followed by three days of festivities.

Narbonne, Fair, with attractions, during October.

Carcassonne, Fair, with attractions, end of November.

Marseilles, the Santon Fair, all December. " Santons " are the little coloured clay figures with which the Christmas crèches are peopled, and thousands come from far around to the Fair to purchase them. Over the years a multitude of purely local figures have been added to the ones of the Biblical narratives, dressed in the costumes of old Provence. These gaily coloured clay figures (the clay is not baked) have a naïve grace. They are the work of a score of local families; moulds and models have been handed down from father to son since the 17th century.

VERSAILLES FOUNTAINS

These celebrated fountains in the gardens of the Palace of Versailles play on certain days during the summer, usually around 4 p.m., and the full display lasts for an hour. There is also a Night Fête at the Neptune

Fountain, at nightfall, on certain dates. It includes the sounding of hunting horns, the play of the fountains, ballets, and a firework display. For current dates enquire from one of the Paris Hostess offices.

WINE AND FOOD FESTIVALS

France is the land of good food and good wines, so, as one would expect, there are many festivals to celebrate these two important gifts to the art of pleasant living. There is not a region of France, in fact, which does not boast delicious specialities, using the local products of the farm, the hunt, and the stream, and all harmonising perfectly with the wine or cider of the countryside.

An outstanding event is the **" Trois Glorieuses "**—three days in honour of wine, held on the Côte d'Or in mid-November. It takes place in three centres: Nuits-Saint-Georges, Beaune and Meursault. On the first day, at Nuits-Saint-George, the Chevaliers du Tastevin in red robes and square toques receive the new members. (The " Tastevin " is a little silver cup from which one tastes wines.) At the ensuing Pig Dinner the animal is served in every possible way and a thousand bottles of wine are uncorked. The Cadets de Bourgogne male chorus entertain the diners with old Burgundian songs.

The second day, at Beaune, there is a sale of wines of the Hospices de Beaune. Dinner by candlelight is held in the Bastion of the Hospice. The third and final day, at Meursault, is, by an old tradition, linked with the newly fermented wine. All those who have taken part in the work of the vineyard and the vintage are invited to a banquet. One hundred bottles of Meursault are given to the winner of a literary competition.

Also in November, there is the **Gastronomic Fair** held in Dijon, when the best in foods and wines for which Burgundy is famous is offered.

Elsewhere in France, there are the **" Beating of the Bounds "** at Pauillac-Medoc in the Gironde, and at the Saint-Emilion vineyards of Saint-Emilion by the Jurade. Both events take place at the end of September. Earlier in the year (early August) there is a **Wine Fair** in lovely Colmar, a fascinating town with many art treasures. At Biarritz, in early June, there is the **National Congress of Gastronomic Confraternities and Wine Jurades.** Macon, too, holds its **National Exhibition of the Wines of France** in May. The display of the great vintages gives this fair a special attraction. Saumur has its **Wine Fair** in February, while even Montmartre has its **Vintage Festival,** for they still crop there the last remaining vineyard within the boundaries of Paris, in an enclosure in the Rue des Saules—but this festivity (during October) need not be taken too seriously.

CHAPTER NINE

Germany

IF YOU LIKE YOUR FOLK STORIES AND HISTORY TO COME TO life, colourfully and lustily, you'll like Germany. Gay historic pageants, authentic costumes and all, make stages out of entire towns, with the populace enacting the rôles of their ancestors in the rousing manner that testifies to the simple pleasures in everyone.

Parades, complete with band music and accompanied by much wine and beer drinking, celebrate every possible occasion. Customs and superstitions arising hundreds of years ago in out-of-the-way communities are commemorated in song and dance with faithful attention to the original details. And with true German hospitality and traditional *Gemütlichkeit*, visitors are warmly welcomed to all these festive occasions which follow the calendar throughout Germany.

Finally, mention must be made of the various excellent musical festivals, many of them performed under idyllic conditions. And there is something to suit every taste: from Wagnerian operas to jazz festivals.

AGRICULTURAL, HORTICULTURAL AND LIVESTOCK SHOWS

The outstanding agricultural show in Germany is the **Green Week** held annually (about the end of January) in Berlin. It draws farmers from all parts of the country as well as from abroad, acquainting them with the latest results in science and research. The exhibition is organised in close co-operation with the West German Federal Ministry for Agriculture and Forestry. Among the exhibits are farm animals and agricultural machinery of every kind, and there is also a flower show, luxuriant in spring flowers.

Every two years there is a **Federal Garden and Horticultural Show.** It takes place in the odd years, and the venue changes.

Other annual flower shows include: **Flower Show in Baroque,** Ludwigsburg (near Stuttgart); **Herrenhausen Gardens** at Hanover, and the **Planten un Blomen** exhibition at Hamburg. Dates can be obtained from the German Tourist Information Bureau.

CARNIVALS

More than any other European country, Germany is the land of Carnival. Each region has a different name for this revelry; each town its own special customs. Munich is the heart of the Bavarian **Fastnacht**— the " eve of fasting-time "—while in the Rhineland there are many ancient traditions observed. Ingenious masks and beautiful costumes are worn at the many carnival balls which are held, as well as at the processions which reach their climax on **Rose Monday,** the day before Shrove Tuesday which marks the ending of the modern Saturnalias.

Starting officially on the eleventh day of the eleventh month of the previous year, the extended festivities end just before Ash Wednesday and need careful planning. There are a Carnival Prince and Princess to be chosen, and these two individuals have to work hard in maintaining the honour, for they are expected to take part in most of the festivities. As an idea of their scope, it may be mentioned that in Munich alone, over 400 Carnival balls are held. Juries, too, have to decide which floats shall be admitted to the processions. Each year fresh carnival songs, many with lilting, haunting tunes, are composed. The outstanding festive carnivals are those held in Cologne, Düsseldorf, Mainz, Münster and Munich, and there is also a big celebration in Berlin. But you will also find much jollity in the smaller towns and villages, and every foreign visitor is warmly welcomed to the jollifications. I myself possess several *ordern* (orders) presented to me by the Carnival Prince at the balls I attended, with a kiss in each case from the Princess. But if your time is limited, then I suggest you attend the Rose Monday celebrations in one or other of the cities I have mentioned. They are certainly unequalled for general merrymaking, as well as being artistically pleasing.

Coopers' Dance, Munich. Every seven years the Coopers' Dance, a 500-year-old custom, is performed in Munich (the next occasion will be February, 1963). It inaugurates the carnival season and lasts to its end. In the city of beer, the coopers have always enjoyed great respect. The dance is performed by 25 coopers, colourfully clad and skilfully swinging hoops of fir branches, beating time to a strange music with their tools on the barrels. The measured movements of the Coopers' Dance are also part of the puppet play seen daily at 11 o'clock by the city hall tower. Individuals, clubs and other organisations may order a Coopers' Dance, and during the carnival weeks, hundreds of orders come in which cannot all be filled. According to tradition, the first is performed on Epiphany in front of the Minister-President's office building. Thousands of people in the street see the dance, and the ministers watch it from the balcony.

The Bell Ringers of Mittenwald. " Bell ringing "—*schellenruehren* in German—is the climax of a colourful masquerade week winding up the carnival season and culminating on the Thursday before Carnival Sunday—for ages called " Nonsense Day." Around noon, the masquer-

aded groups of the various trades meet amidst a constant " *Joho, Joho,*"
the carnival call of Mittenwald. Shoemakers and coopers enjoy the
privilege of measuring the girls for shoes and crinolines, playing practical
jokes in the process. They are followed by masked figures wearing
multi-coloured " patch-garments," with bells on them. And across the
market square moves the " old-women's mill "; old women are dumped
in at the top and gay lovely young girls emerge at the bottom. After a
while, a mighty singing and tinkling of bells is heard from the distance.
The first man to appear is a huge mountaineer in leather shorts and a
wide, embroidered leather-belt from which dangle 16 bells. He is the
leader of the " bell-ringers " and is followed by identically equipped
companions. It requires great skill and strength as, continually jumping,
they move in carnival procession, every step and jump evoking a harmonious accord in a definite rhythm.

CULTURAL EVENTS

In almost every town in Germany you will find some musical or
dramatic festival, and I recommend your studying the current year's
" Calendar of Events." Here I can only mention a few of the more
important occasions:

International May Festival (opera and drama), Wiesbaden,
during May.

For lovers of **Chamber Music** and Baroque Architecture, the
concerts in the long gallery of mirrors and state rooms in Herrench emsee
Castle, built by Ludwig II of Bavaria, will be of interest. From May to
September, every Saturday night, the gallery is lit with 4,000 genuine
candles, and lends an atmosphere which will long be remembered.

Mozart Festival, Würzburg, mid-June to early July, and held in
the Residenz.

Europe Weeks (operas, drama, concerts), Passau, two weeks in
June-July.

Opera Festival, Coblence, July 1st to mid-September. This has
a rather unique theatre where a floating stage is set up on the Rhine,
while thousands of spectators sit on the banks or drift lazily around the
stage in boats.

Luisenburg Festival (open-air), North Bavaria, July-August.

Bayreuth Festival,* end of July to end of August. The most important music festival in Germany is that held in the Festspielhaus in
Bayreuth. This is, of course, the mecca for lovers of Wagner's operas.
As hotel accommodation is rather limited in this town, it is worth noting
that arrangements are made for the transportation of visitors staying
in Nuremberg. The theatre in Bayreuth offers the last word in modern
production, and when you are there I hope you may get the opportunity
to attend a performance in the small opera house of the Margraves, a

little gem of a building whose interior is decorated in a perfect baroque style.

International Bach Week, Ansbach, late July and early August.

Opera Festival, Munich, mid-August to mid-September.

Beethoven Festival, Bonn, first two weeks in September.

Festival Weeks, Berlin, two weeks in September-October.

Modern Music Festival, Donaueschingen, early October.

Open-air Opera and Operetta Performances at the Red Gate, Augsburg.

On the " Romantic Road," between Rothenburg-ob-der-Tauber and Nördlingen, lies the ancient little town of Feuchtwangen. Its Romanesque Cloisters form an impressive background for the **Festival Plays** which are performed there every summer.

Among other **Open-air Drama** festivals are those at Schwäbisch-Hall, where the stage is the lovely flight of steps of St. Michael's Church in the medieval town square ; the castle courtyard at Jagsthausen ; at Bad Gandersheim/Harz; and at Bad Hersfeld (near Fulda).

For those interested in films, the outstanding event is the **Berlin International Film Festival,** late June to early July.

While illuminations and fireworks may hardly be classed as cultural, yet I will mention them here. **The Rhine Aflame** at Coblence is an exciting display of illuminations and fireworks; it takes place in mid-August; also at St. Goar in mid-September.

The largest **Fireworks Performance** occurs, however, at Constance, on Lake Constance, in mid-August. And meriting mention are the **Illuminations** at Herrenchiemsee Palace, from May to September. Also to be noted are the illuminations of the ancient castle at Heidelberg— three times during the summer.

Peasant Theatres in Bavaria. Peasant theatres, all with a tradition of hundreds of years, are flourishing in many communities in Bavaria. The country-stages of Lake Schliersee and Tegernsee, where amateur actors have gradually developed into professionals, have become famous the world over, but even smaller stages, like the ones at Kiefersfelden or at Flintsbach in the Inn valley, offer a fine sort of native dramatic art. Originally, religious plays were performed. Later on, the romantic life of knights and robbers found favour, a still very popular subject. There are plays with such promising titles as " The Avenger at the Dead One's Coffin " or " Siegfried and Lumilla, or the Punishment and the Recovery of Geroltsburg Castle Ruin," and " Almanses and Elvira, or From the Slave Market to the Throne." Most plays are full of casualties and the swords clang heavily together. Delightful involuntary jokes amuse the listener. It is hard to describe and it must be seen to be appreciated.

Flintsbach tackles pieces like " Ben Hur." It is dreadfully exciting to hear the roar of the lions which the young actors have rehearsed so earnestly. Other peasant stages are, of course, dominated by home-grown subjects and dialect poetry/plays with Alpine backgrounds interspersed with songs and costume dances.

Comparatively new among the Bavarian folk festivals, but neverthe-less highly impressive, is the colourful **Song Festival** held each Whitsun-tide at Aschau in the Chiemgau in Upper Bavaria. It was held for the first time in 1938 and has quickly developed into an all-Alpine inter-national affair in which singing and dancing groups from Bavaria, Austria, and Switzerland participate. The contests—the festival is largely a matter of competitive performances—include such typically mountaineer features as yodelling, clog dances (the famous *schuhplattler*), alpenhorn blowing, and flag swinging. All participants appear in their picturesque native costumes, of course.

At Bad Aibling, Rottach-Egern on Lake Tegernsee, and other towns in southern Bavaria, **Alpine singing contests** and **folk festivals** have also been arranged recently during the summer months.

RELIGIOUS EVENTS

The outstanding religious event in Germany is the **Oberammergau Passion Play** which takes place every 10 years. The next occasion will be 1970. This wonderful dramatic presentation of Our Lord's Life and Crucifixion dates back to 1634, when it was first staged in fulfilment of a vow made by the inhabitants that if they survived the plague they would re-enact the sufferings of Christ every 10 years. At that time, the population of Oberammergau was little more than 700 souls.

With very rare exceptions, and then only because of disturbed conditions such as wars, the Passion has continued through the centuries. While in the past the number of performances was limited, in 1960, the last occasion, 85 performances were given, attracting 500,000 visitors. The present modern theatre, seating up to 6,000 persons, was specially built in 1930. There are no artificial lighting effects, and while the auditorium is covered in, the stage is quite open.

An indication of the scope of this enterprise is shown by the fact that the parish has now available more than a thousand valuable costumes, the majority of which are made from real and rare Oriental materials and give a fine colourful effect. Only persons born in the village may take part in the play, and both men and women let their hair grow for years in advance. Although certain criticisms were made regarding the last presentation, it is to be hoped that this historic event will not suffer from being too much modernised, thus detracting from its original purpose and spirit.

Procession of Light, Pottenstein, January 6th (Epiphany). A highly impressive religious festival is celebrated in this little town in the Franconian mountains of northern Bavaria. " Closing festival of the Eternal Adoration " it is called, and consists of a grand " Procession of Light." Prior to the event, logs are carried to the rock summits for use as giant bonfires. On Epiphany day, triumphal arches and small altars are erected in the streets of the town, Christmas trees with candles are placed around house doors, and wreaths are deposited around the statues of saints. In the late afternoon, while the town's bells ring, a procession makes its way through the town, while at the same time bonfires flare up on the mountain tops and rocks. The dominating castle is floodlit, star shells rise in the wintry sky, torch-bearers hustle around, songs and sacred music fill the air. The town, in fact, seems to be a grand sea of flames, an unforgettable sight, especially when snow covers the landscape. A solemn divine service in the town church ends the Procession of Light.

Adorning the Fountain, Franconian Mountains, Easter. Often called Franconian Switzerland, wells on the lonely plateaus are the object of special attention and of demonstrations of gratitude at Eastertide. They are then festively adorned with small pine trees from which bunting flutters. This custom, dating back to pagan times, is closely connected with the rejuvenation of nature at this season of the year.

In some Franconian villages, another custom is added: the wells and fountains, besides being decorated, undergo a thorough cleaning and polishing. On the Saturday before Easter or in the early dawn of Easter Sunday, water is fetched from the wells to be sprinkled on the fields so that no harm may befall the growing harvest. " Easter baptism," the procedure is called. In some towns and villages, in Gosberg in the lower Wiesent valley, for instance, the peasant women take home, after divine services, the " Easter-blessed," consisting of a piece of ham, eggs, salt, bread, and baked lamb or hare meat.

In Niedermirsberg, near Ebermannstadt, Easter bonfires are lit in front of the church on the Saturday before Easter. The charred sticks are taken home for good luck.

St. George Ride, Effeltrich, April 23rd. This colourful celebration in honour of the patron saint of the church of Effeltrich in eastern Franconia is always the occasion of a magnificent display of peasant costumes. In the forenoon, the young men gather on horseback between the thousand-year-old linden tree and the church yard. After High Mass, the cavalcade forms and, headed by a rider on a white horse, bearing a standard, moves off to marching music. The cavalcade rides around the church and farms. After its return to the linden tree, a wide circle is formed around the clergyman who, after a speech from horseback, blesses horses and men. A second procession follows in the afternoon in which the entire population joins. The young girls proudly display

their tall tinsel crowns while the older women wear an artistically tied
and embroidered white head-cloth.

Corpus Christi Procession, Lake Chiemsee. Many thousands
of people take part in this solemn boat procession which starts from the
venerable cathedral of the Frauenwörth Monastery on Frauen Island.
The participants board gaily-decorated boats, circle the little island in
four stages, and return to the cathedral while bells ring and boellers
(small mortars) boom. At the four ends of the island, the four gospels
are sung. The blessings are accompanied by shooting and dipping of
the flags.

Seehausen on Staffel Lake also has its **Lake Procession.** About 100
boats and barges follow the decorated ship carrying the Holy of Holies,
stopping at St. Jacob and Wörth islands.

St. Gregory Festival and **Flinderer,** Pegnitz, three weeks after
Whitsun. Situated at the eastern entrance to the Franconian mountains,
this little town celebrates the festival of its patron saint with a merry
festival. There are games and all kinds of entertainment and merrymaking, while the children's part is shared by enthusiastic older people.

St. Gregory's day is usually followed by another holiday, when
the local inns hold what are called " flinderer " days, during which
especially strong beer is on sale. There is also much to eat in the way
of *metzel* soup and all kinds of pork dishes. Those entitled to hold the
" flinderer " announce the fact by planting a hop stalk in front of the
house door. On such days, Pegnitz is the magnet for people from towns
many miles around.

St. Ulrich Ride, Steingaden, Sunday preceding or following July 4th.
A cavalcade in honour of the Saint's name-day is staged around Kreuz-
berg Church at Steingaden, between Oberammergau and Füssen. The
peasants in this Alpine foreland region are experienced horse breeders
who adorn their horses artistically. The mane is entwined with ribbons
or with straw or dressed with tow in a long plait, while the young men
wear eagle feathers on their hats.

St. Anna Festival, Franconia, July 26th. In Forcheim, St. Anna's
Day is a great folk festival, when tens of thousands of visitors attend to be
merry, drink beer, sing songs, and enjoy a grand time. Among the
festival's features, which is perhaps more secular than religious, is the
annual main shooting contest of the Forcheim marksmen's guild.

Another **Annafest,** but more of a religious character, takes place at
the same time in Waischenfeld, at the north-east entrance to the Franconian Mountains district. It is the result of a vow made over a century
ago—a vow which the people believe to be the reason why they are spared
heavy thunderstorms. Whenever a thunderstorm is threatening, they
still pray: " Saint Mother, Anna, drive the storm asunder."

Christmas Festivals. Christmas is celebrated with great zest in

Germany, and every town and village is gaily illuminated and decorated, with Christmas trees much in evidence. Perhaps you get the true spirit best in one or other of the smaller villages. But among the major celebrations the **Christkindlesmarkt** of Nuremberg is undoubtedly the most impressive. The principal reasons are that only such things are permitted to be offered for sale as are directly connected with Christmas, and that the entire structure of this festival is based on artistic good taste. As a result it provides a unique attraction, attended by guests from many countries. The main market square is the excellent setting, in view of the famous Schöner Brunnen (Beautiful Fountain) and the 600-year-old Frauenkirche—Our Lady's Church.

The festival lasts three weeks (from early December to Christmas), and the mayor and town council take part in the opening ceremonies. The mart is inaugurated by choral singing and trumpet melodies from the church gallery, where a child dressed as the Christ Child and two leaf-gold angels pronounce a rhymed invitation to visit the Kris Kringle's Mart. The ringing of church bells, Christmas carols, fairylike illuminations, artistic decorations and some ten thousand children are parts of the touching spectacle. The entire mart centres about a large Christmas crib in the market square. Medieval lanterns, artistic signs, sheds, pavilions, and booths—all in uniform Christmas style—and, last but not least, the scent of goodies and fried sausages—combine to give the scene its characteristic atmosphere. It is like a scene from the Arabian Nights.

Shortly before Christmas a candlelight procession of Nuremberg children carrying home-made lanterns moves through the city. Daily round trips by romantically decorated horse-drawn post coaches are made. This festival has a history of more than 400 years, and in the 16th and 17th centuries foreign royalties and their suites came to admire and enjoy the unique event.

Star Singers, Bavarian Alps, New Year's Day or Epiphany. This is one of the most beautiful customs in the region. The group is headed by a man carrying on a long pole the " great star," brightly lighted from within. On it, little Jesus and other religious motives are painted. Behind the star-carrier march the " Star Singers " who are followed by the entire village. At all important buildings and squares they stop to sing the old star carols—melodies and words sometimes dating back to the 16th century.

While the custom is generally practised on Epiphany, Oberammergau has for centuries advanced it to New Year's Eve, and many visitors join the procession of villagers which lasts several hours. The songs review events of the year that has passed and extend good wishes for the one to come. In the Passion Play village an entire band—selected members of the Passion Orchestra—marches along in the procession. Magnificent voices are heard and many a head seen that is familiar from the Oberammergau stage and choir. At the same time the youth of Oberammergau are on the march, costumed, with the " little star." Their orchestra is but small: a few violins, a bass viol and a guitar.

Wedding Customs in Germany. In almost every part of Germany, especially in the rural districts, traditional wedding customs are still observed. It is true that many a custom today seems ridiculous and without sense. Yet some of them can be traced back to their original Germanic meaning, like the choice of Tuesdays and Thursdays for wedding days. These days were devoted to the Gods by the old Germans. Noisy wedding-eves and screaming during the bride's reception were meant to scare away demons and witches. The " robbery " of the bride on the morning of the wedding day originates from the old custom of bride-robbing. Feeding of cats by the bride has its origin in Germanic tradition, too: cats were the favourite animals of Goddess Freya, the Nordic Goddess of love.

The opportunity to witness an unusual wedding ceremony is, of course, a matter of chance. But I give here brief notes on wedding customs in various parts of the country.

Eastern Frisia. Here you may find a triumphal arch erected in front of a wedding mansion.

Northern Frisia. An old " witch," usually a neighbour and cook of the wedding dinner, refuses entrance to the young couple, using a big broom. She admonishes bride and bridegroom to keep an honourable and faithful marriage. Only after they have promised to fulfil all the wishes and conditions of the old " witch " is the bridegroom given the key to the house and permitted to enter with his wife. A triumphal arch may be erected in front of the house where the wedding party will take place. At the wedding party many jokes are played on the young couple including fastening a buggy on the top of their new home.

Nordmark. In some villages a wooden goat—symbol of fertility—is carried, with musical accompaniment, to a house where the next wedding will take place, or to the home of a bashful bachelor who ought to be encouraged. The wooden animal is then " fed " and " watered." The person honoured this way invites the party into his house. In some villages, bones of the wedding dinner are brought to the next house, whose receiver invites the people inside. At Finkenwerder, some colourful wedding customs are still observed.

Westphalia. Century-old wedding customs survive in this part of Germany. Frequently, the bride receives a wedding cap and the bridegroom a slipper at midnight. In the Munsterland, the bride's veil is torn at midnight. In some villages, young men put a buggy and a stork's statue on top of the house or they decorate the roof with baby clothes. In Geerde (near Münster) the entire neighbourhood engages in joyous festivities on the wedding eve. In some villages, too, shots from mortars are fired throughout the wedding day. Hagen, Nordenau and Afelderbach are three Westphalian villages noted for special customs.

Weserbergland. The bride's veil is " danced out " after the wedding dinner: the bride's friends try to tear off a piece while the bride is anxious to preserve this veil. In some parts of the Weser Forests, a rope with baby's clothes is drawn in front of the wedding mansion. The young couple must remove all these before they are allowed to enter. Wedding parties in the Weser Mountains last frequently two or even three days, starting at 9 a.m. Guests who have not arrived by this hour are fetched, sometimes in wheelbarrows and even only dressed in a nightgown. Male guests who come unshaved or late are plastered with a painting brush full of whipped cream and are shaved with a huge wooden knife. During this procedure, they have to drink a large glass of vermouth on an empty stomach.

Weser Forests. In the Schaumburg district in case the bride has an unmarried older sister, she has to dance around in a pair of wooden shoes. There are other curious customs in this area.

Harz. Traditional costumes are worn at weddings, even in the cities like Goslar. On returning to the wedding mansion from the church, bride and bridegroom are required to saw a log in front of the house. This is supposed to be a symbol for all grief and happiness the married couple will bear from now on.

Lower Rhine. On the Sunday of the second wedding announcement in church, friends and relatives of the bridegroom visit him in his home to " comfort " him, with many drinks. At the same time, the bride is carried around by neighbours in a basket as a symbol of her farewell to her former kind of life. There are many other strange wedding customs in this part of Germany, some of which are quite comical. The wedding-bed, for instance, may have peas spread between the sheets, while even a hedgehog, a live cock, thistles, or bottles of wine may be placed there. There are also some rough customs.

Rhineland. In some districts colourful folk costumes are worn. The smashing of pottery on the wedding eve is popular, and the bridegroom or the bride's father must clear away the rubble.

Swabia. Here one does not marry " below one's class." Sometimes a professional marriage-negotiator is employed by parents to effect satisfactory negotiations. These embrace adequate dowries, while everything for the wedding is strictly determined in advance. The entire village joins in the subsequent festivities.

Black Forest. More serious formalities are required here. Some amazing costumes, and more particularly headgear, are to be seen. Bridesmaids, for instance, in St. Georgen have hats that resemble small Christmas trees, measuring a foot in height, another foot in width, while the hat is strung out with gilt, tinsel, and glass balls. The bride's bonnet differs only in height, width and general splendour, for flowers and blown-glass fruit are often added to the colossal edifice, and, as a last incongruity, apart from the formal dress coats and silk hats of the accompanying males, the bride wears a white ruff from which two wide ribbons fall over a bosom upholstered with velvet, chains and embroidery. The wedding goods (dowry, furniture, seeds, spinning wheel and cradle) are trans-ported on a decorated wedding carriage. Young boys salute the pro-cession by shooting anything that makes a noise.

Not every day is considered proper for a wedding, but Tuesdays or Thursdays, the days of the old Germanic gods, are regarded as suitable. At some places in the Black Forest, the bride puts consecrated salt and herbs into her shoe before going to the church; and during the ceremony both try to step on each other's foot, for the one who steps first will be the ruler in the future marriage. After church the young couple may walk to the graves of their parents (if deceased) to ask for their blessings—they are " invited as guests " is the saying.

Swabian Allgäu. Much eating and drinking are features at Swabian weddings. Experienced guests bring little baskets or sacks with them in which they put everything they cannot manage to eat. In the middle of the feasting, the bride may disappear, for she is " stolen." Robbers and bride eat and drink in another inn of the village for as long as the desperate husband and his friends have not yet discovered them. Another original custom is only rarely practised today: a race competition with wheel-barrows to the church.

Bavaria. No German district has so many wedding customs as Bavaria. An attractive feature is the *Kuchlwagen*, a farm wagon colour-fully painted and drawn by the farmer's best horses. It is packed with the bride's furniture, always including a cradle, and it journeys to the future home of the young couple. Both men and women wear the traditional dress of their district. The girls are very elaborately garbed, and in some villages of Lower Franconia the bride has to wear at least seven slips if she wants to go " stately." In the mountain villages, friends steal a load of hay during the ceremony from the stables of the bride's parents, which is piled up in front of the church as a symbol of luck. Exactly on midnight, the young couple are " blown out " and receive a farewell with music and good wishes. There are many other curious customs to be found in Bavaria, but space does not allow me to develop this interesting theme further. You could always enquire at the local tourist office about any wedding taking place, and might arrange to be present.

Northern Eifel. An old custom is a kind of trial marriage. On the eve of May 1st, the boys of a village, full of drink, go to a nearby hill and call out couples in a " May-marriage." After this, they must date each other. Frequently, as one might expect, real weddings develop from these funny "marriages." Among the wedding customs, in the districts of Kaltenherberg, Hofen and Hohren, the neighbours put barricades in front of the couple's new home. Only after everyone is given a drink are these barriers lifted.

Hesse. In the districts along the rivers Lahn and Dill, young boys crack whips to greet the married couple. More fun is carried out by tooting on watering-cans and by beating the big lids of pans. In some Hessian villages, young hemlock trees are put in front of a bride's house on her wedding day. Northern Hesse is noted for its traditional folk costumes and hair arrangements. Many ancient traditions are still observed in the country villages.

Franconian Switzerland. Another area where practical jokes are the order of the wedding day. Wedding crowns are often worn. The cook burns an apron in the kitchen, for this is believed to bring fortune to the young couple.

Eastern Franconia. To safeguard a bride on her way to the church, the bridegroom arranges for strong " Stutzer-riders," armed with swords, to accompany her. This applies only in those cases where the girl comes from another village to the bridegroom. Later, at the wedding feast these guards push their swords into the ceiling above the head of the bride in order to have them easily available.

PILGRIMAGE CENTRES

Cologne. Germany's most famous five-nave cathedral, built between 1248 and completed only in the 19th century, in Gothic style. It contains the valuable shrine with the bones of the Magi. Pilgrimage dates: Corpus Christi.

Kevelaer. This is the most famous pilgrimage centre in North Germany. It is dedicated to " Mary, the Consoler of the Distressed." Every year it attracts over half a million pilgrims. Pilgrimage dates: May 1st-October 31st (every weekday except Friday).

Deggingen (Wurtemberg). The miraculous picture of " Ave Maria " is to be seen in the pilgrimage church which dates from the 18th century. Pilgrimage dates: throughout summer, notably on Sundays and holidays.

Würzburg. The chapel high above the town is the Franconian pilgrimage centre, for it contains the miraculous picture of " Our Lady of Sorrows." Pilgrimage dates: no set dates.

Bogenberg (near Straubing). Close to the banks of the Danube, the Church of Our Lady has a piece of the True Cross which attracts many pilgrims. Pilgrimage date: Whit Sunday (candlelight procession).

Schonenberg (near Eilwangen on the Jagst); the church is a great achievement of German late-baroque. Pilgrimage dates: no set dates.

Maria Laach. The Benedictine Abbey on the Laacher Lake in the

Eifel has a Basilica consecrated in 1156. It is a pearl of Romanesque architecture. But it is not really a pilgrimage centre.

Mariahilf (Passau). The veiled picture of Mary, " the Source of True Help," is enthroned in a fine little baroque church on the heights above Passau. Pilgrimage dates: mid-June.

Neviges. The pilgrimage centre of Hardenberg-Neviges, in which Our Lady of Neviges has conquered the hearts of the Rhinelanders. Pilgrimage dates: May 1st-November 5th (daily except Fridays and Saturdays).

Dreifaltigkeitsberg (near Speichingen). Pilgrimage dates: no set dates.

Fulda. St. Michael's Church is the oldest in Germany dating from the time of Charlemagne. Pilgrimage dates: no set dates.

Bornhofen (Middle Rhine). The church dates back to the Middle Ages and is a place of pilgrimage dedicated to Our Lady of Sorrows. Pilgrimage dates: no set dates.

Andechs. The magnificent rococo church houses precious relics from the times of the Crusades including three holy Hosts. Pilgrimage dates: Ascension Week and on Sundays (June-October).

Werl (Westphalia). A miraculous work of art depicting Our Lady and the Holy Child—known as the " Consoler of the Troubled "—was carved in the 12th century. It is the centre of religious life in Westphalia. Pilgrimage dates: May-October, with special celebrations early July.

Blieskastell (Saar). The Chapel of the Holy Cross has a miraculous picture of the Black Madonna of the Arrows, which has been venerated since 1243. This is the most frequented pilgrimage centre in the Saar and the Rhine Palatinate. Pilgrimage dates: mid-March to mid-August (various dates).

Frauenchiemsee. A Benedictine nunnery on an island in the middle of Lake Chiemsee. It is famous for its Corpus Christi procession on the lake in boats. Pilgrimage date: Corpus Christi.

Weingarten. The ancient Benedictine Abbey is a gem of baroque architecture. The Procession of the Holy Blood held annually since 1090 is a famous pilgrimage event. Pilgrimage dates: on " Blood Friday," following Ascension Day, there is the " Blutritt " procession across the fields.

Ettal. A white marble statue of the Virgin is greatly venerated. The village lies near Oberammergau. Pilgrimage dates: dates change each year.

Aachen. Many important relics, among the richest north of the Alps, are in the Cathedral Treasury. Pilgrimage dates: no pilgrimages, but every seven years (1965 is the next occasion) the " Heiligtumsfahrt " (Pilgrimage to the Holy Relics) takes place.

Birkenstein. The highest pilgrimage centre in Bavaria, at the foot

E

of the Wendelstein close to Miesbach and the lovely baroque church of Fischbachau. Pilgrimage dates: changeable each year.

Wies. This pilgrimage church is perhaps the loveliest building of its kind and size in the world. It has been called the " Throne Room of the Lord " on account of its wonderfully beautiful interior. " The Pilgrimage to the Flagellated Saviour " attracts great crowds. Pilgrimage dates: March 19th, Easter Monday, Whit Monday, July 25th, first Sunday in September, and second Sunday in October.

Maria Eich (near Munich). Amidst lovely oak woods, the pilgrimage church is dedicated to Our Lady, and is very popular. Pilgrimage dates: mid-April to end September (various dates).

Vierzehneiligen. A Franconian pilgrimage centre, with a large church dedicated to the 14 Saviours. It is a masterpiece of rococo. Pilgrimage dates: no set dates.

Altotting. This is Bavaria's most famous pilgrimage centre and dates back to Carolingian times. The " Chapel of Mercy " is dedicated to the Black Virgin. The Collegiate Church has a rich Treasury and the tomb of the great Marshal Tilly. Pilgrimage dates: mid-March to end October.

Trier. Last, but certainly not least, is the world-famous pilgrimage centre of the " Holy Mantle." The Cathedral is one of the oldest churches in Germany, and its Treasury contains the Holy Mantle of Christ. Among the Roman relics are a huge amphitheatre and the famous Porta Nigra. Pilgrimage dates: no set dates.

SPORTING FIXTURES

Motor racing is a popular German sport, and many important events take place at the 14-mile Nürburgring in the Eifel (in the triangle between Coblence, Trier and Cologne). The main event is Germany's **Grand Prix,** which is held during the first week in August, and it is one of the major events that contribute points to the annual world championship.

Other important motor racing events are:

Rhein-Pokal Race (for motor cycles), Hockenheim, second week in May.

International 1,000 km. Race for Sports Cars, Nürburgring, late May.

Grand Prix, Berlin, late June.

International Solitude Races, Stuttgart, late July.

Horse racing is popular, too. Notable events are the **German Derby** in Hamburg at the end of June, and the **Iffezheim Week** at Baden-Baden, at the end of August.

Gliding is another favourite in Germany, and there are several gliding clubs and courses, particularly at Hornberg, Unterwössen and Wasser Kuppe.

For winter sports, the main centres are Garmisch-Partenkirchen and Oberstdorf. The outstanding events at these and other resorts will be found in the annual " Calendar of Events." The Feldberg (near Freiburg) is the site of the **Black Forest Ski Championships** (late February), while in the Harz Mountains there are special ski and toboggan competitions at St. Andreasberg and at Hahnenklee-Bockswiese.

Amongst water sports, the following events are specially worth noting:

International Motor Boat Racing, Traben-Trarbach (Moselle), end of May.

Sailing Regatta, Hamburg, early May and early October.

Sailing Regatta, Borkum island, early June.

International Sailing Week, Kiel, June.

International Rowing Regatta, Mannheim, mid-June.

International Rowing Regatta, Mainz, second half of June.

An unusual sport is the **Schütüenfeste,** an ancient target practice. Important events are at Goslar (Harz Mountains) in July, at Schliersee (Bavaria) in late July, and Xanten (Rhineland), late July and early August.

TRADE FAIRS

Many trade fairs of international repute are held in Germany throughout the year. A full list of these is published by the German Tourist Information Bureau and further information can be obtained from numerous fair representatives in the United Kingdom. Situated in the heart of Europe and easily accessible from all parts of the world, the trade fair towns of Frankfurt, Hanover, Cologne, Munich, Nuremberg and Offenbach in effect form one big trading centre of outstanding importance. Although marked by their own individuality, the trade fairs complement each other both as regards the goods they display and the type of visitors they attract, thus creating a central meeting place of international trade for producers and buyers from all continents; 745,000 square metres of space are available to the exhibitors at the six biggest German Trade Fairs. Last year some 20,000 exhibitors—22 per cent. of them coming from abroad—displayed their products at the German Trade Fairs to buyers from 105 nations: an almost inexhaustible opportunity for comparison of some of the best achievements in production and supply.

The approximate dates of the six most important German Trade Fairs held regularly are:

International Household Goods and Hardware Fair, Cologne, early Spring and Autumn.

International Toy Fair, Nuremberg, early Spring.

International Leather Goods Fair, Offenbach, early Spring and Autumn.

International Frankfurt Fair, early Spring and Autumn.

German Industries Fair, Hanover, end of April to early May.

International Handicrafts and Trade Fair, Munich, end of May and early June.

TRADITIONAL CUSTOMS

Meistertrunk* (Master Draught) and **Shepherds' Dance,** Rothenburg-on-Tauber, Sundays in June, July and August. The Meistertrunk is the best known and most popular of the Bavarian history plays. And it takes place, of course, in perhaps the most picturesque medieval town in Germany. " The Master Draught " is based on chronicled events of the Thirty Years' War. When, in October, 1631, the Imperial Field Marshal Tilly brought his troops to the town, demanding its surrender, the citizens refused. However, at last they had to give in, and the conqueror decided the burgomaster and the councilmen should suffer the death penalty. Pleas from the women and children softened Tilly's heart somewhat. But good wine did more, for when he saw the magnificent state beaker he stated that if the burgomaster or one of the council could empty it at one draught all should live and the city be spared. Burgomaster Nush undertook the task, and emptied the beaker at one draught, thus saving everyone.

This historical beaker is still used when the epic story is re-enacted to-day, although this scene is but one in a play in which the actors wear period costumes. The entire town is the stage, with the troop encampment outside the city walls, the children's plea with Tilly on the market square, and all the rest.

In the afternoon of some days of the history play, the historical shepherds' dance is performed in the market square. It is danced in honour of St. Wolfgang, patron-saint of shepherds, and commemorates a member of the shepherds' guild who made a race from his pastures to the city to bring warning of the approach of an enemy. The troop encampment outside the city walls lasts until late, when camp fires and torch-light add to the romantic scene. On certain evenings during the summer, Hans Sachs plays are given in a local hall.

Kinderzeche (Children's Feast), Dinkelsbühl, July. This medieval town, not far from Rothenburg, also re-enacts an episode from the Thirty Years' War. When a Swedish colonel came with his troops to conquer the town, the burghers were split in their attitude. In perplexity the city fathers tried vainly to find a solution. Ruin and destruction seemed inevitable. It was then that a beautiful young girl, named Lore, accompanied by a crowd of small children, offered to go out to meet the Colonel and to beg pity for the town. But before the plan could be realised the Swedish troops had entered the city, ready to destroy it. At that moment, the song of children's voices sounded from afar, and then Lore appeared with her young band. Fearlessly she faced the conqueror, knelt and begged his mercy for the town and its people. The colonel's heart softened, and Dinkelsbühl was saved from destruction.

The Kinderzeche festival is first of all a children's event. It usually begins on the Saturday before the third Monday in July with beer sampling on the " shooting meadows." The next morning the boys' band marches through the city in historical costumes, playing lustily. The festival play is performed in the ancient market hall. During the play period, the entire town is one great festival ground. There are processions, children's dances, concerts, guild and sword dances, and many other entertainments.

Hamelin is mainly familiar to us through the legend of the **Ratten-fänger** (Rat-catcher), related in Browning's poem. The event is cele-brated each Sunday in summer when the story is re-enacted by a piper and boys, the latter disguised as mice. Unfortunately, modern research tends to discredit the legend, claiming that what really happened was a visit from a labour agent who attracted many local young men away to Bohemia, with the promise of good wages.

The Princely Wedding,* Landshut, every two or three years (usually on three Sundays in June and July). This is one of the most colourful events in Europe. It is a re-enactment of a gorgeous wedding which took place in 1745 when Ludwig the Rich married his son, Duke George, to Hedwiga of the Royal House of Poland. In addition to a festive procession, the houses of this medieval town are beautifully decorated for the occasion, and nearly a thousand " burghers," dressed in the rich costumes of the Middle Ages, strut around and bring those opulent days back to life for a short while. I say " opulent," for it is officially recorded that at the feasting which followed the actual wedding, 333 oxen, 275 fat pigs, 40 calves, and 12,000 geese were eaten.

Tanzel-Festival, Kaufbeuren, July. This is another outstanding costume festival held in a small town lying between Augsburg and Füssen. It celebrates an old custom dating back to 1497, and begins with the enactment of an historic scene, when the burgomaster with his councillors receives King Conradin who, on horseback and accompanied by his knights and bishops, appears at the door of the town hall. The festival's climax, however, is the great procession through the town, with heralds, flower-girls, drummers, the King, the city council and their ladies, lansquenets in plus-fours, followed by the guilds and their state carriages, among them weavers, brewers, tanners and blacksmiths. Archers appear, flag-wavers, medievally-clad soldiers and yellow mail coaches with postillions industriously blowing their horns. There are many bands, while perhaps the most beautiful features of the festival are the 800 children, dressed in historic costumes.

Anno 1634, Nördlingen, during summer months. This is the most southerly of the three medieval towns lying on the " Romantic Road," and it still retains its fortress wall with 18 towers. The Daniel Tower of its fine St. George's Church still sees a unique nightly ceremony, for at nine each night a watchman at its summit cries to another on the ground that " All's well." The play re-enacts various events in the Thirty Years' War. There are dances in period costumes, concerts and other entertainments. The town's populace form the cast for the play, and the streets offer a fascinating picture, resembling indeed a medieval master's painting.

Spearing the Dragon,* Fürth-im-Wald. For 500 years this town in the Bayerischer Wald has performed an exciting open air play (every second Sunday in August), called " Drachenstich " (spearing the dragon). It is based, obviously, on some pagan legend. Performed in the market square, the play has as its climax the killing of the dragon (50 ft. long, 10 ft. high, and weighing over a ton) by a knight on horseback who pierces the monster's head by thrusting his spear into it through the throat. The hero must be careful, however, not to miss a pig's bladder filled with ox blood, so the wounded animal can spout blood. The dragon looks comically gruesome when it spouts fire, rolls the eyes, shows its giant teeth, wiggles its large blood-red tongue and twists its huge body. With the Drachenstich, of course, go merrymaking and various festivities, including a grand procession through the streets.

Fürth-im-Wald is also the scene of a Leonhardi Ride—a religious festival really, and it takes place on Easter Monday. Other Leonhardi Rides in Bavaria are usually held on November 6th, the saint's day.

Trenck, the Pandur, Waldmünchen (July to August). This open-air play performed after dark is notable for its excellent artistic management and the highly realistic acting. Among the players are many direct descendants of the characters they represent in the play. The story is about the capture, sack and burning of the town by a notorious leader of Hungarian Pandur bands in the year 1742. The nightly troop encampment scenes, wild riding, and especially the storming of the town with scaling ladders, torches and burning pitch, are exciting and exceedingly well done.

Ulmer Fischerstechen, Ulm, first Monday in August on the Danube. According to old tradition, two boats approach with the participants in old costumes, and try and joust each other into the water with lances. The " sport " was already popular in the 16th century when Kaiser Karl V and his son, later King Philip II of Spain, allowed it in 1549. This *Turnier auf dem Wasser* (tournament on the water) was played in the old Ulm days when it was a free city and the game took place between youngsters of the fishermen's guild. It is today performed as a pageant, and is also popular in other countries.

Potters' Festival, Passau, first Saturday in August. The products of the potters of the Ilz section of this three-river city have long been famous. Although their great boom period is no more, the Ilz "Haferl Festival" (pottery festival) is still celebrated with great enthusiasm. All the buildings in town and the moated castle, Niederhaus, are specially illuminated, dance music is played in the open, there are open-air performances, water games, boat racing, and a pageant. The climax is a large scale illumination of the town and Oberhaus fortress and the old section of Passau. There is a splendid display of fireworks; and one seems wafted to a night in Venice.

Folk Festival, Nuremberg, usually in August. Founded in 1826, this festival is rather similar to the better-known Oktoberfest of Munich. There are the great beer tents, representative shows, entertainments and other attractions. On the Friday before the first festival Sunday the chief burgomaster empties the first " mass " (about one quart) in the course of a grand beer sampling ceremony. Crowds pour into the city from the surrounding Bavarian towns and villages, and there is a joyous atmosphere of wit and good humour—two strong characteristics of the citizens.

Teenagers' Festival, Worms, first week in September. This is one of the most amusing festivals in Germany. Among the events are the historical coachmen's dance, a hilarious fishermen's jousting tournament on the Rhine, fought from small boats, a parade of illuminated vessels, and a giant firework display. Huge wine and beer tents, holding thousands of visitors, as well as numerous booths are to be found in the fair grounds beside the river's bank.

The Tura Michele, Augsburg. Since 1526, a group of figures representing the archangel Michael with the Devil at his feet has been in the understructure of the Perlach Tower of the city hall. On St. Michael's Day, September 29th, the angel appears every hour on the hour, and with each sound of the hour stabs the struggling Devil. During the last war the historical figure was destroyed, but a new one is now carrying on the old custom. Every year a fair is held on this day and the so-called " Tura Michele " is visited by many tourists.

Driving the Cattle Home, Bavarian Alps. According to an ancient custom the *almabtrieb*—driving the cattle home from the mountains—is the occasion of a great autumn festival in the Bavarian Alps. In a festive procession the cattle, wreathed and garlanded, stamp down the hills, the dairy maid out front and the shepherd boy following the herd. Particularly pretty is the driving-down of the cows from the pastures above Lake Königssee near Berchtesgaden, where the cattle are carried across the lake by boat.

Traditional Costume Festivals, Southern Bavaria. The " Union of Bavarian Costume Clubs " comprises some 650 clubs with a total of 70,000 members. Throughout the year, but especially during the summer months, these clubs hold costume festivals.

One of the outstanding examples is the **Annual Pageant** in Munich in October.   The most beautiful native costumes from all over the country are on parade there, to the accompaniment of bands, also in native garb.   These costume days and festivals are real folk events, complete with field mass, extended processions, honour dances, and music band contests.

Leonhardi-Ride, Bad Tölz.   November 6th is the name-day of St. Leonhard, patron saint of the horses.   In Old Bavaria, the day has been observed for centuries by the peasants' " Leonhardi Ride " to church in which well-groomed, beautifully harnessed horses draw richly decorated wagons.   While many villages have clung to this ancient custom, no Leonhardi Ride has become so famous as the one of Tölz in the Isar river bend.   The preparations take weeks, and from distant farm-steads they come to Kalvarien (Calvary) Mountain at Tölz, high above the Isar.   There, since 1722, a chapel stands on the spot where a huge old tree used to grow.   Singing and praying, the picturesque procession of about 60 wagons moves three times around the little church.   At the end of the ride the young men stage a contest in whip-cracking—an art which is held in high esteem.   November 6th is a big day for the Tölzer riflemen's band, for they accompany the main procession with smart marching tunes.

The Buttenmandl Custom, Berchtesgadener Land.   In two town-ships of the Berchtesgadener Land, the " Buttenmandl " custom is still practised in the original form as recorded in 1642.   It is observed annually in Loipl in the evening hours of the first Sunday in Advent, and in Winklon the second Sunday.   The word " butten " means " shake," namely, shake up to new strength.   There are 12 " buttenmandl " (little butten men) under a " master ";   also one Santa Claus with two " Krampus," or devils, accompanying him, and all curiously dressed.   They assemble outside the town, and, after " shaking " bells and praying, the " Butten-mandl " run together to certain homes where they must be admitted. There they pray and make much noise with their chains and bells to drive out evil spirits.   The ceremonies end with unmasking.

Hat-Singing, Dachau.   In Dachau, near Munich, " hat singing " is a very ancient custom.   It is a winter-time habit which serves to shorten the long nights, and is performed in public.   The singers have to ponder over a riddle which is proposed in rhymed song and to which they have to sing the answers also in rhymes.   Thus, Bavarian wit and characteristic love for beautiful folk melodies are reaping a great harvest.   In Old Bavaria the hat is the sign of manliness, and so the prize for hat-singing in the beer halls is—a hat.

Berchten-Runners and the Twelve Nights, Bavaria.   Recently, many Old Bavarian Advent customs, neglected during the war, have been revived.   They originate from pagan usage and conceptions later adapted into Christian customs.   So, for instance, the " Berchten-running " during the Advent season, has been revived in many Bavarian localities. The " Berchten-runners " wear frightening masks. In Upper Bavaria women mostly lead the procession, carrying chains, brooms and pick-axes. This custom, no doubt, once centred around Frau Berchta who, in German lore, was at the same time the benign goddess of light and a gruesome figure of frightful appearance. She punishes the tardy at the spinning wheel, but she also makes the fruit grow in the fields. Therefore the " Berchten-runners " go from farm to farm demanding a tribute in the form of little presents.

On St. Barbara's Day the farmer's wife cuts cherry buds which will be in full bloom at church-night.

Deepest magic, however, hold the 12 nights between Christmas and Epiphany and particularly the three preceding nights of December 21st, Christmas night and Epiphany eve. Ancient superstition has it that fates are decided on these nights, and so the lead is cast to unveil the secrets of the future or to win future's favour.

Christmas Shooting, Berchtesgaden. On Christmas Eve and New Year's Eve, no fewer than 1,200 marksmen go to the 15 shooting ranges located high above and around the Berchtesgaden valley. Each time, the shooting around midnight lasts about an hour. At 20 shots to one pound of powder, and about a ton and a quarter being used up, that makes 70,000 shots ! The echo from Watzmann, Hoher Goell, Jenner, Untersberg and other mountain giants increases the effect of the thundering noise terrifically.

The custom is very carefully cultivated by 15 Christmas Shooting Clubs in the " Berchtesgadener Land." It undoubtedly goes back to the time immediately following the invention of black powder and derives from the still older custom, of heathen times, of driving out evil spirits by din and noise.

The Berchtesgaden Christmas shooters shoot also at Easter, Whitsuntide, during the Corpus Christi Procession, and at major family affairs of their members. The clubs wear their picturesque old costumes, and include veterans among the *boellerers* (gunners) who are known all over the country for their originality and particularly their huge round beards. A treat to the eye also are the riflemen's hats of green velour with a flowing chamois beard, marksman's cord, and a revolving chamois wheel.

A VARIETY OF CELEBRATIONS

In the spring, for instance, **Killing the Winter** ceremonies are held in many communities. Winter, an ugly straw puppet, is carried out of the village on a long pole and either burned or drowned, to the accompaniment of shouting and beating of drums and kettles.

A spectacular **Easter custom** is the rolling of flaming wheels down the hillsides on Easter Sunday night. Giant oaken wheels, seven feet in diameter and weighing around 800 lb., are tightly stuffed with straw, set afire and rolled down the hill into the valley as thousands of watchers gathered around bonfires on neighbouring hilltops cheer. If the wheels are still burning when they reach the valley, it is regarded as a good omen.

In the Harz Mountains they still celebrate **Walpurgis Night** on April 30th, when witches flying from the Brocken (the highest mountain in North Germany, but in the Eastern Zone) are driven out in noisy pitched battles, and the people who aid the good spirits will be rewarded with good crops and other good fortune during the coming year. Braunlage, Torfaus and Bad Harzburg are three centres for these festivities, although there is a tendency nowadays to lessen their former rather pagan atmosphere.

Among the other North Bavarian folk festivals, I list the following:

St. Kunigund Festival, Lauf-on-Pegnitz, first Sunday in July.

Wallenstein Festival, Altdorf, July and August.

The Honey Shooter, Feucht.

The Fasalecken, Baiersdorf.

Kermis, Fürth.

Shepherds' Festival, Hersbruck, January 6th (Epiphany). (This town has the only shepherds' museum in Germany.)

Mountain Kermis, Erlangen.

Waberla Kermis, Ehrenburg Hill.

Pumpkin Festival, Muggendorf (Franconian mountains), last Sunday in September.

St. Stephan Ride, Moggast, December 26th.

Pretzel-and-Beer Week, Creussen.

St. Georgi Ride, Gunzendorf, April 23rd.

Whitsun Wedding, Kotzting.

Kermis, Lindentree, on the Sunday of, or before, August 24th.

The Rattler Boys, Bamberg, Holy Week.

Historical Fête, Kronach, Sunday after Corpus Christi.

Historical Play, Rötz, in medieval rock castle.

Play about Princely Honour, Parsberg.

Epicure Festival, Buchel Stone (between Deggendorf and Grafenau), to commemorate an old hermit, June 16th (or the Sunday following).

The Rehabilitation of Dr. Eisenbarth, Viechtach (historical play). There is also a weekly celebration (during summer) at Hannoversch-Münden in the Weserbergland.

WINE AND BEER FESTIVALS

During the autumn months (late August until the end of October), a large number of merry **wine and vintage festivals** are held in all the picturesque little towns along the Rhine, the Moselle, Ahr, Nahe, Main, Neckar, Danube and many other wine growing districts, including those in the Lake Constance district.

Among the best-known of these festivals are those held daily at Coblence at the Wine-Village, at Rudesheim, Bingen, Boppard, Bernkastel, and Traben-Trarbach. At Ingelheim there is a claret festival, and the Niederdollendorf wine festival includes an historic marksmen's procession. In the Rhine Palatinate, along the " Wein Strasse," Bad Dürkheim stages every year a traditional sausage market linked with Germany's largest wine festival, while not far from there, at Landau, there is a flower pageant in conjunction with the wine celebrations. Then, at Neustadt, the wine festival includes the election of the German and Palatinate wine Queens, and the christening of the new vintage, and, last but not least, a colourful vintners' procession.

Many more of these outstanding festivities could be named, like the cuckoo mart at Eberbach on the Neckar, the autumn wine festival at Heilbronn, and the festival at Weinsberg with the historical play " The Women of Weinsberg."

No mention of German jollifications can omit the **Oktoberfest** held each year in Munich—in late September and early October. For 16 days thousands of visitors from all over the world will join the gay company and join in all the fun of the fair. There are processions and pageants, and almost unbelievable quantities of food and drink are consumed. On the 150th anniversary of this festival, for instance, the record was: nearly three million quarts of beer, 6,600 quarts of wine, over 6,000 quarts of spirits, 247,000 cups of coffee, 213,000 chickens, 740,000 pairs of pork sausages, 92,000 pairs of beef sausages and 97,000 lb. of fish.

For the current year's dates of festivals, apply to the German Tourist Information Bureau. And remember that, however " sticky " you may be at home, when you join in a wine festival you will certainly find that you " let your hair down " and that you will be assured of a hearty welcome.

CHAPTER TEN

Gibraltar

THIS BRITISH OUTPOST AT THE SOUTH-WEST EXTREME OF EUROPE has the advantage of being an ideal centre from which to do shuttlecock trips into both Spain and North Africa. In many other respects, it will seem home-from-home to the British visitor—with the notable exception of the weather, which is glorious most of the year !

Apart from the occasional **Ceremony of the Keys,** which takes place at sundown just within the Inner Gates of Gibraltar with typically British pageantry, there are two recently established annual festivals which will most likely be repeated in future years.

Arts Festival, held from May 24th to June 3rd in 1961. The programme includes something of everything, ranging through music, drama, films, sports, pottery, painting and photography. An interesting feature is the use of St. Michael's Cave as a natural concert hall; this is the largest cave in the Rock, about 1,000 feet above sea level, liberally embellished with stalactites and stalagmites.

Week of the Sea, held from July 29th to August 6th in 1961. Rowing and yachting regattas, swimming contests, international deep sea fishing competitions and under-water fishing are included in the programme.

CHAPTER ELEVEN

Great Britain

FEW PEOPLE WILL ARGUE WITH ME IF I SAY THAT BRITAIN OF all countries in Europe has the pomp and ceremony of tradition the most deep-rooted in her daily life. Events such as Changing the Guard and the Ceremony of the Keys are an integral part of London day-by-day—even if visitors tend to appreciate them more than Londoners themselves! On a grey November day, tradition on a grand scale colours the City streets on the occasion of the Lord Mayor's Show, while quaint traditions survive in every part of the country throughout the year.

Amongst our cultural activities, the Edinburgh Festival in the late summer is known all over the world; leaving London aside, world-famous actors and musicians can be seen at some time or other at smaller festivals in nearly every provincial town.

Sports lovers will find something of everything in the way of international events. To any visitor to Britain, however, whether sports loving or not, I strongly recommend a leisurely summer's afternoon at almost any village cricket match. There he will step into a scene more typically British than on any sports ground of international fame.

AGRICULTURAL, HORTICULTURAL AND LIVESTOCK SHOWS

Annual Bull Shows and Sales, Perth, February. The two main events are: for Aberdeen-Angus bulls (early in the month); Shorthorns (middle of the month).

Cruft's Dog Show, London, February. Britain's biggest canine gathering.

Badminton Three-day Horse Trials, Badminton, Gloucestershire, end of April.

Chelsea Flower Show,* London, mid-May.

Royal Ulster Agricultural Society Annual Show and Industrial Exhibition, Balmoral, Belfast, end of May.

Royal Windsor Horse Show, Windsor, towards mid-May.

Richmond Royal Horse Show, Richmond, end of May.

Bath and West and Southern Counties Show (agricultural), different venue each year, end of May or early June.

71

Royal Highland Show, Ingliston, near Edinburgh, June. Scotland's biggest agricultural show.

Three Counties Show (agricultural), Malvern, Worcestershire, mid-June.

Royal Show, from 1963 annually at Stoneleigh, near Kenilworth, July. England's biggest agricultural show.

Great Yorkshire Show (agricultural), Harrogate, mid-July.

The Royal International Horse Show, London, end of July.

Shrewsbury Musical and Floral Fête, Shrewsbury, Shropshire, mid-August. Perhaps the biggest floral event in Britain.

Southport Flower Show, Southport, Lancashire, end of August. Biggest flower show in the north of the country.

Royal Horticultural Society's Great Autumn Show, London, end of September. This society also holds fortnightly shows during most months of the year. Their lovely gardens at Wisley, Ripley (Surrey) are open to the public on weekdays.

Horse of the Year Show, Wembley, Middlesex, early October.

Annual Dairy Show, London, end of October.

Smithfield Fatstock Show and Agricultural Machinery Exhibition, London, early December.

CULTURAL EVENTS

Shakespeare Season of Plays, * Stratford-on-Avon, beginning in March or April, for about eight months. The fine, modern Memorial Theatre on the banks of the River Avon in Shakespeare's home town is recognised as Britain's premier theatre for Shakespearean productions. Some of the leading actors and actresses in the profession take part.

Pitlochry Drama Festival, Pitlochry, Perthshire, mid-April to end of September. The Festival Theatre is set in the heart of the Perthshire Highlands and programmes range from modern to classical, including foreign and Scottish plays of distinction.

Royal Scottish Academy Annual Exhibition (Art), Edinburgh, end of April to mid-August.

Royal Academy Summer Exhibition (Art), London, early May to mid-August.

Glyndebourne Festival Opera, * Glyndebourne, Sussex, end of May to mid-August. One of the leading musical festivals in the world, both for its quality and beauty of setting. The opera house was built by the founder of the Festival, Mr. John Christie, C.H., together with Audrey Mildmay, Mrs. Christie, in the glorious gardens of his ancestral Tudor home. Meals are available during the very long interval, but, for many members of the audience, one of the features of the Festival is to picnic in the lovely surroundings. As evening dress is recommended, the whole occasion has the graciousness of a past age.

Aldeburgh Festival, Aldeburgh, Suffolk, June. A varied 10-day programme of opera, chamber and classical music, lectures, poetry-reading, exhibitions and drama includes the works of Benjamin Britten, who has made this ancient borough his home.

Bath Festival of the Arts, Bath, for ten days in May or June. The programme, under the artistic direction of Yehudi Menuhin, includes music (particularly featuring the works of J. S. Bach), ballet and drama, and a Festival of Jazz.

York Mystery Plays and Festival of the Arts, York, three weeks in June and early July, every three years. The world-famous York Mystery Plays are performed in the ruins of St. Mary's Abbey. The programme also includes some first rate music, poetry, lectures, drama, art exhibitions. It will next be held in 1963.

Chester Miracle Plays, Chester, every five years. The oldest of the four surviving medieval cycles of plays will next take place in 1962.

" Sound and Light " Performances, near Henley-on-Thames, end of June and early July. An excellent attraction against the romantic background of Greys Court, founded in the 13th century.

Cheltenham Festival of British Contemporary Music, Cheltenham, two weeks in early July.

Llangollen International Musical Eisteddfod, Llangollen, one week in July. Singers and dancers from many countries compete at this event.

Harrogate Hallé Music Festival, Harrogate, one week in July. Evening concerts by the famous Hallé Orchestra range from Beethoven to Gershwin.

Haslemere Festival of Early Music, Haslemere, one week in July. Early music is played on the instruments for which it was written and which are still made in this small Surrey town.

Royal National Eisteddfod, different centre each year in Wales, one week in August. A competitive festival of music, drama, literature, arts and crafts, chiefly famous for the glorious singing of the renowned Welsh choirs.

Edinburgh International Festival of Music and Drama, * Edinburgh, end of August and early September. Amongst the leading cultural festivals in the world for music, grand opera, ballet, drama and including the superb Military Tattoo. The **International Film Festival,** held during the same period, includes a number of world premières.

Three Choirs Festival, held in rotation at Hereford, Gloucester and Worcester in that order (1961 at Hereford), one week in early September. Main performances still take place in the cathedrals, whose choirs originated the Festival in the early 18th century.

Coventry Festival of Music, Coventry, one week in October. Includes conductors, orchestras, and soloists of international fame.

National Gaelic Mod, different centre each year in Scotland, one week in October. A great Gaelic festival of music, poetry and the arts generally.

Cheltenham Festival of Art and Literature, Cheltenham, usually first two weeks in October.

Swansea Festival of Music and the Arts, Swansea, a week in October. Programme includes concerts by world-famous orchestras.

RELIGIOUS EVENTS

Blessing the Throats, St. Etheleda's Church, Holborn, London, February 3rd. A survival of a ceremony introduced to Britain over a century ago, in which two long candles tied together in the form of a cross are held under the chin of those suffering from throat afflictions.

Blessing of the Sea, Hastings, May. In this Rogationtide custom, the Bishop of the Diocese blesses the fishermen and their nets from the seashore, after a procession starting from churches in the town.

SPORTING FIXTURES

Opening of the Flat Racing Season and the **Lincolnshire,** Lincoln, towards end of March.

Grand National* (Steeplechase), Liverpool, March.

The Boat Race, Oxford v. Cambridge, River Thames (Putney to Mortlake), March or April. Perhaps Britain's most " national " boating event, since nearly everyone in the country is an ardent supporter of either the dark blue of Oxford or the light blue of Cambridge.

2,000 Guineas and **1,000 Guineas,** Newmarket, April. This is Newmarket's first Spring Meeting of the flat racing season.

Marble Championships, Tinsley Green (Sussex), Good Friday.

Football Association Cup Final, Wembley, early May.

Rugby League Cup Final, Wembley, mid-May.

The Derby* and **The Oaks** (flat racing), Epsom Summer Meeting, end of May to early June.

Royal Ascot (flat racing), Ascot, mid-June. The most fashionable horse racing event of the year.

International TT Motor Cycle Races, Isle of Man, mid-June.

Amateur Championship (Golf), different place each year, towards end of June.

International Clyde Fortnight (Sailing), Firth of Clyde, June. Regattas at many centres.

Forth Week (Sailing), Granton, June.

Test Matches (Cricket), England v. Australia, five events during June, July and August, every four years in Britain. Matches are held at Lords, The Oval, Old Trafford, Leeds and Birmingham or Nottingham. Last held in Britain in 1961.

The Championships* (Lawn Tennis), Wimbledon, end of June to early July. Perhaps the most important event of its kind in Europe.

British Lockheed International Aerobatics Contest, Coventry, early July. The contest for the **King's Cup** takes place at the same time.

British International Grand Prix (Motor racing), Silverstone, Northamptonshire, mid-July.

Henley Royal Regatta, (Rowing), Henley-on-Thames, July.

Open Championship (Golf), different place each year, July.

Sheep Dog Trials, July and August. Perhaps the most interesting of these are the national events held annually in England, Scotland and Wales. **International Sheep Dog Trials** take place in September at a different place each year.

Cowes Week (Sailing), Isle of Wight, end of July to early August. Most fashionable event of its kind in Britain.

Manx Grand Prix Motor Cycle Races, Isle of Man, early September.

Greyhound St. Leger, Wembley, early September.

St. Leger (Flat Racing), Doncaster, September.

Farnborough Air Display,* Farnborough, early September. Biggest event of its kind in Britain.

Ryder Cup Matches (Golf), Great Britain v. U.S.A., October, alternate years in Britain. Held here in 1961.

Cesarewitch (Flat racing), Newmarket, October.

Cambridgeshire (Flat Racing), Newmarket, October.

News of the World Relay Race, London-Brighton, October. Similar events are also arranged in other parts of Britain.

November Handicap (Flat Racing), Manchester, November.

Royal Highland Gathering (Highland Games),* Braemar, early September. Though this is the biggest event of its kind, mention should be made of the Highland Games which take place annually at Dunoon, Aboyne and Oban between end of August and mid-September. Indeed, similar events of a more local nature occur in one centre or another virtually every Saturday during the summer.

R.A.C. Veteran Car Rally, London to Brighton, November. An astonishing variety of ancient models are entered annually by their proud owners. The event was started in 1896.

TRADE FAIRS

International Boat Show, London, January.

Daily Mail Ideal Home Exhibition, London, March.

Antique Dealers' Fair and Exhibition, London, June.

International Motor Show, London, October.

F

TRADITIONAL CUSTOMS

Changing the Guard, London, throughout the year. Most visitors to London place this near the top of the list of things to see, and indeed it is a ceremony dear to the hearts of even the most country-bound Briton. The days can vary, but in principle you can see it every morning at 11.30 before Buckingham Palace or St. James's Palace. Mounting the Guard at the Horse Guards, Whitehall, is a daily event at 11.30 a.m. (Sunday, 10 a.m.) and features alternately the two regiments of the Household Cavalry: the Life Guards in red tunics and the Royal Horse Guards in dark blue.

Ceremony of the Keys, * Tower of London, throughout the year on written application to the Resident Governor. Every night, the Tower of London is ceremoniously locked up—it is, in fact, the only night-time ceremony remaining in London, and occurs during the seven minutes or so before 10 p.m. You can see the four bearskinned guards waiting to escort the keys, the unarmed soldier carrying an ornate candle-powered lantern, and the warder who then accompanies them to lock the gates of each tower. At the Bloody Tower, a sentry challenges the detail. Responding to " Halt, who goes there ? " the answer comes, " The Keys." " Whose keys ?," " Queen Elizabeth's keys," " Advance Queen Elizabeth's keys. All's well." It is all beautifully timed to end just before the hour strikes and the Last Post sounds.

Andrew's Dole, Bideford, Devon, January 1st. When John Andrew died in 1605, he left a will stating that the rent of a plot of land should be set aside for the relief of the poor and aged. The dole, distributed annually on January 1st, works out at approximately 1s. a head, but a further £2 is now provided by the Corporation of the Borough and distributed in the form of loaves of bread.

Annual Dicing for the Maid's Money, Guildford, Surrey, January. An unusual form of " gambling " takes place every year at the Guildhall, presided over by the Mayor. The Maid's Money is the proceeds of various charitable bequests which have been made in the past, and competitors for it are chosen for their long domestic service in the Borough. Oddly enough, the loser gains a more valuable bequest than the winner ! The ceremony is open to spectators.

Haxey Hood Game, Haxey, near Doncaster, January 6th. In the 13th century, the hood of a lady out riding was blown away and promptly chased by 13 men in attendance. The incident has given rise to a primitive form of rugby in which 13 men take a principal part—the Fool, the Lord and 11 Boggins, who act as supervisors. The Fool begins by making a speech, to be shouted down by the crowd (known as " smoking the fool "). The crowd, divided into two groups, each with a goal, which is one or other of the two village inns, battles with several canvas hoods until eventually a piece of leather or the " hood " is hurled into the game. It must be carried to one of the goals where free drinks are served on the house until 6.30 p.m.

Up-Helly-A,* Lerwick, Shetland, last Tuesday in January. It means " End of the Holiday " and is a survival from the occupation of the Shetlands by the Norseman. There is an impressive torchlight procession and a 30-foot model Viking galley is carried through the town by the " Guizers," finally to be burned. Revels and dancing continue long into the night.

Hurling the Silver Ball, St. Ives, Cornwall, first Monday in February. The origins of this very old custom are unknown. At 10.30 a.m., the silver ball is thrown from the wall of the Parish Church by the Mayor, to be caught by one of the waiting children and adults, and passed from hand to hand on the beaches and in the streets of the town. Whoever holds it at noon receives a reward of 5s. on presenting it to the Mayor at the Guildhall. About the size of a tennis ball, it is made of wood covered with silver-leaf.

Olney Pancake Day, Olney, Bucks, Shrove Tuesday. The pancake race has taken place annually at Olney for over 500 years and is the most famous of several such races which occur on this day. Only women are eligible, and they must wear an apron, head-covering and carry a frying pan in which the pancake must be tossed three times in the course of the race. The winner is rewarded with a kiss from the vicar. Pancake eating throughout England on this day goes back to the times when people went to confession and were shriven before Ash Wednesday, the first day of Lent. Since eggs and butter could not be eaten during this period, any supplies were used up in the making of pancakes on the eve of Ash Wednesday.

Shrovetide Football, Ashbourne, Derbyshire. One of the best known of several such events which also occur in Alnwick, Northumberland, and Sedgefield, Durham, on Shrove Tuesday. The goals are three miles apart, and the football and players, whose number is unlimited, invariably pass through a number of streams before a goal is scored.

Whuppity Scoorie, Lanark, March 1st. One story concerning the origin of this custom concerns an English soldier who, escaping massacre by Wallace and his men, sought refuge in the church. As there was some delay in opening the doors, he had to circle the church three times crying " Sanctuary," still hotly pursued by Wallace's men crying " Up at ye "—possibly accounting for the corruption " Whuppity Scoorie." Today it is the custom for children swinging paper balls to circle the parish church.

Midgley Pace Egg Play, Mytholmroyd, Hebden Bridge, Midgley and Luddenden, Yorkshire, Good Friday. The word pace comes from " pasch " or " pâque," and the event bears a resemblance to the Christmas mumming plays. A constant struggle between good and evil is personified by St. George and the villain Toss Pot. Other characters include the King of Egypt, the Bold Slasher, the Black Prince of Paradine and the Doctor. The players are boys of Calder High School, Midgley, in the West Riding, who dress in colourful costumes and paper head-dresses.

Bread and Cheese Distribution, Biddenden, Kent, Easter Monday. The Biddenden Maids, Eliza and Mary Chulkhurst, were Siamese twins born in 1100. On their death in 1134, they left their property to the poor of Biddenden, and a dole of bread and cheese is still distributed annually from the Old Workhouse. Since 1907, the Trust has been extended to include gifts of money, nursing and treatment for the sick.

Hungerford Tutti-Men, Hungerford, Berkshire, second Tuesday after Easter. At Hocktide, the Tutti-men, or " tything men," go from house to house, exacting money from the men and kisses from the girls. In return, the people of Hungerford are given oranges, distributed by an " orange-scatterer " in a hat bedecked with feathers. The two tutti-men, wearing morning coats and top hats, carry poles adorned with posies, and an ancient horn is sounded from the balcony of the Town Hall. The ceremony commemorates the granting by John of Gaunt of free fishing rights on the river Kennet and free use of the common lands of Hungerford.

St. George's Court, Lichfield, April 23rd. At noon on St. George's Day, is held the Ancient Court of the View of Frank Pledge and Court Baron of the Burgesses within the Manor of Lichfield. It has taken place continuously since Norman times, but today it is the Town Clerk who presides as Steward of the Manor. A jury is empanelled to hear complaints and to appoint two High Constables, two Pinners and a Bailiff. Many of the people who attend wear a rose.

Shakespeare Birthday Celebrations, Stratford-on-Avon, April 23rd. Townspeople and distinguished visitors go in a procession to lay wreaths on the grave and to visit Shakespeare's birthplace. The town itself is decorated with flags and bunting.

Hobby Horse Display, Minehead, May 1st. The custom of carrying the decorated hobby horse through the streets of Minehead is probably a survival of an ancient fertility rite. The " horse " is more than six feet long, made of canvas and decorated with ribbons. It makes various appearances and dances through the streets on May Day and the two following days, to the accompaniment of drums.

Padstow Hobby Horse Day, Padstow, Cornwall, May 1st. Padstow's " Obby Oss " may have originated in the 14th century as a scare against raiders. Today, he dances through the decorated town, enticed by his " teaser." A black hoop covers the man underneath, and he is crowned by a grotesque mask.

Riding the Bounds, Berwick-on-Tweed, Northumberland, May 1st.

This ancient ceremony is said to date from an Anglo-Scottish truce in 1438, when the ten-mile boundary was defined. At 11 a.m., a cavalcade sets off from the Parade, followed at 11.30 by the Civic Party in a motor coach. Riders and Civic Party enjoy light refreshments at the " Corporation Arms " on the way, and the ceremony ends as the party returns to the Town Hall.

Helston Furry Dance,* Helston, Cornwall, May 8th. This gay holiday—adopted by the church on St. Michael's Day, for he is Helston's patron saint—was most likely a pre-Christian Spring Festival. The town band begins to play in the early morning, but the principal dance takes place through the decorated village streets at noon. Men wear morning dress, women long dresses, and the catchy music may well lead their dancing feet in and out of shops and houses.

Court of Arraye, Lichfield, Whit Monday. The Court of Arraye of Men and Arms is said to date back to the 15th century, when Lichfield was compelled to supply armour for the nation's defence. The armour was paraded annually for inspection, and the custom is revived today on Whit Monday, when the young lads of the town appear before the officials in coats of mail, many of which are of ancient origin.

Skye Week, Isle of Skye, one week in May. Celebrated by special events in many places throughout the island.

H.M. The Queen's Official Birthday—Trooping the Colour,* Horse Guards Parade, London, June 10th. A splendid pageant in which the Colour is trooped by the Brigade of Guards before the Queen. But get there early if you want a good view.

Riding the Marches or **Common Ridings.** Every border town has its own ceremony, but the two main events are held at Selkirk and Hawick in June. Riding the Marches or " redding the marches " was introduced in the Middle Ages, when it was often necessary to rectify boundaries destroyed by fire. Originally this took place as the need arose, but later occurred at regular intervals. In Selkirk, the event is combined with celebrations commemorating the Battle of Flodden. The Royal Burgh Standard Bearer leads a cavalcade of some 200 riders round the marches of the Common Lands, and on their return to the Market Place there is a colourful ceremony known as Casting the Colours.

Welcome Week, Isle of Arran, one week in June. Celebrated by a variety of special events.

Royal Tournament, London, June. Superb displays by the Armed Forces.

St. John's Eve Chain of Bonfires, many centres in Cornwall, end of June. The custom of lighting bonfires on hilltops was a pagan ritual, later adapted in honour of St. John. They are ceremoniously lit at about 10 p.m. after a signal received from St. Ives. Words in Cornish are pronounced and a bunch of flowers thrown into the fire. In some cases,

young couples jump through the fires, following a superstition that if
they do they will be married before long. Fires are lit in: St. Ives,
Penzance, Helston, Camborne, Redruth, Truro, St. Austell, Liskeard
and Callington.

Doggett's Coat and Badge Race, River Thames (London Bridge
to Cadogan Pier, 4½ miles). Held under the auspices of the Worshipful
Company of Fishmongers, this is the oldest established annual event on
the British sporting calendar. Its founder in 1716, Thomas Doggett, an
Irish comedian from Dublin, died in 1721, leaving in his will a legacy
to provide annual prize money and a special coat and badge for the
champion oarsman of the Thames. The Doggett coat is reddish orange,
tight-waisted and full-skirted, and is buttoned down the front.

Tynwald Ceremony, Isle of Man, July 5th. This ancient open air
assembly of the Manx Parliament takes place every year on old Midsummer's Day on a circular grass mound at St. John's. New laws are
proclaimed in both English and Manx, whose strong Scandinavian
character is an effective reminder of Viking associations with the island.
Representing the British Government, the Lieutenant-Governor of the
Isle takes the central seat occupied by the Norse king, the Bishop at his
side, with the two Deemsters, or Manx Judges, and members of the
Legislative Council, roughly equivalent to the British House of Lords.
The 24 members of the House of Keys, corresponding to the House of
Commons, sit on the tier below.

Swan Upping on the Thames, London Bridge to Henley, July.
When swans were first introduced into Britain from Cyprus in the
13th century, they were the King's property. Subsequently two City
companies, the Dyers and the Vintners, received the privilege of keeping
swans on the Thames from Queen Elizabeth I, and today all the swans
on the river are still divided between Her Majesty and the two companies.
In July, official swan markers in special uniforms go upstream marking
all the new cygnets on their beaks to distinguish their ownership. This
task takes about one week.

Rushbearing Ceremony, Westmorland. This medieval custom,
which recalls the time when newly cut rushes and sweet smelling herbs
replaced the old ones in the aisles of the churches, is still observed at
Ambleside in July and at Grasmere and Macclesfield in August. The
children carry flowers and garlands in procession through the streets, and
a special service is held in the church.

Battle of Flowers, Jersey, early August.

National Town Criers' Contest, Hastings, Sussex, August. Town
criers, complete with uniform and handbell, come from many towns,
particularly from the West Country. Some of the costumes are of great
historic interest. The same text is read by all the contestants and is
preceded by the traditional cry " Oyez, Oyez."

Piepowder Court, Bristol, September. During fairs and markets of days gone by, disputes were settled at a temporary court known as the Court of Piepowder—the name appears in various forms. The ceremony still takes place at the Tolzey Court in Bristol, when the Clerk and the Sergeant at Mace take their stand on the covered pavement and the Proclamation of the Piepowder Court is read.

The Sheriff's Ride, Lichfield, early September. A charter granted by Queen Mary in 1553 ordained that there should be an annual tour of the limits of the city by the Sheriff of Lichfield on the day of birth of the Virgin Mary. Each year the sheriff and a cavalcade of riders encircle the ancient bounds of the city, halting at various points for refreshment.

State Opening of Parliament,* London, in the autumn—usually late October or early November. H.M. The Queen drives through the streets to the Houses of Parliament in a coach, accompanied by members of the Household Cavalry: the Life Guards and the " Blues."

Guy Fawkes' Day, all over the country, November 5th. On this day in 1605, the conspirator Guy Fawkes attempted to blow up King James I of England and his Parliament. His failure to do so is marked by nation-wide celebrations every year, featuring fireworks and bonfires on which effigies of Guy Fawkes are burned tr umphantly. These " guys " are usually made by the youngsters and displayed on the streets well in advance in the hope that they will raise sufficient funds to buy fireworks. Passers-by are cajoled into a " penny for the guy " or begged to " remember the fifth of November, Gunpowder, treason and plot. . . ." Organised firework displays and celebrations are held in many towns, particularly in Sussex, such as Lewes and Rye. At the Houses of Parliament, there is a ceremony observed before the official opening of Parliament when the Vaults of the House of Lords are searched by the Queen's Bodyguard of the Yeoman of the Guard.

Firing the Poppers, Fenny Stratford, Buckinghamshire, November 11th. Since the church was built in 1730, it has been the custom to " fire the poppers " in honour of St. Martin's Day, though recently this has been done, too, on occasions of national rejoicing. The poppers resemble quart-size metal pots, each weighing about 20 lb. They are charged with " shilling powder " and fired by applying a red-hot rod. To-day, the ceremony takes place on the Manor Fields Sports Ground.

Lord Mayor's Show,* London, second Saturday in November. Perhaps the most colourful of London's annual pageants, the event dates back some 600 years. The Lord Mayor is driven in state in a 200-year-old golden coach from the Guildhall to the Law Courts to take the oath before the Lord Chief Justice and the Judges of the Queen's Bench. His bodyguard is formed by the Company of Pikemen and Musketeers, and a procession of various liveried footmen, coachmen, riders and decorated floats moves with due pomp through the crowded streets.

Closing the Gates, Londonderry, Northern Ireland, Saturday
nearest to December 17th. As the Earl of Antrim marched on Derry
to garrison the city in 1688 in the name of James II, 13 young apprentices
rushed to the Ferryquay Gate, locked it and seized the keys. Thus began
a siege which was to last 105 days. Now, every year the installation of
new boys is held in the Apprentice Boys' Hall and, at 4.30 p.m., an
effigy is burned of Lundy, the traitor and Governor of the City, who was
in favour of surrender.

Tolling the Devil's Knell, Dewsbury, Yorkshire, December 24th.
The birth of Christ means the Devil's death; thus, each Christmas Eve,
the Devil's Knell is tolled at Dunster Parish Church the same number of
times as the numbers of the year (i.e. 1,962 times in 1962). The tolling
starts at 11 p.m., is suspended during the church service from 12 to
12.45, and is then resumed until the years have been tolled away.

Masons' Walk to Melrose Abbey, Melrose, Roxburghshire,
December 27th. Freemasons of the Melrose Lodge gather in the afternoon of St. John's Day to elect their office-bearers and to transact other
business. Since 1707, this has been followed by a torchlight procession
through the town. At that time, it was proposed in the Lodge minutes
that the members " do attend the Grand Master on St. John's Day to
walk in procession from their meeting to their place of Rendezvous . . . and
that each in the company walk with the Grand Master with clean aprons
and Gloves." They are preceded by a silver band as they march in
procession by way of the Mercat Cross to Melrose Abbey.

WINE AND FOOD FESTIVALS

Hotelympia, London, ten days in January to early February
in years with even numbers. Undoubtedly the biggest of its kind in
Britain, this mammoth show devoted to the hotel and catering industries
and the culinary art was established in 1887 and attracts world-wide
attention. Apart from the big trade sections, an important aspect of this
event is the Salon Culinaire, a competitive section for both senior and
junior classes. A Table d'Honneur provides a display of the culinary
achievements of laureates and gold medallists from previous years.

International Gastronomic Festival, Torquay, Devon, end of
April, years with uneven numbers. The brain-child of Mr. Michael
Chapman of Torquay's famous Imperial Hotel, and certainly the leading
international gastronomic event outside London.

CHAPTER TWELVE

Greece

NOW THAT GREECE IS DEVELOPING INTO ONE OF THE POPULAR holiday lands of Europe, it is certain that many of her traditional celebrations will become developed into tourist attractions. At the present time, however, most of the festivals spring from the rites of the Greek Orthodox Church, although there are the important annual drama performances at Epidaurus and Athens. The National Tourist Organisation of Greece issues each year a fairly comprehensive list of " Coming Events."

AGRICULTURAL

There are no agricultural shows of national importance; but mention might be made of a **Strawberry Festival** which is held at Florina, a town of Western Macedonia, where strawberries are the chief farming product, and there is an **Olive Festival** at Kranidion, a borough in the Peloponnese, where olive oil is produced in large quantities. Aegion (north coast of the Peloponnese) stages a **Flower Festival.** In the Easter Season, a **Flower Exhibition** is held in the town of Kalamata, as well as simultaneous nautical festivities.

CARNIVAL

Carnivals are held on the last two Sundays before Lent at both Patras and Athens. The former is by far the most important, however. In this attractive town, capital of the Peloponnese, the festivities start with the entry into the town of King Carnival's herald, who is accompanied by two bands. The following day—a Sunday—King Carnival's float comes along, to be followed in the evening by a grand parade, with the float, groups of artists and others in fancy dress. After this start, there is a week of parades and masquerades, dances, merrymaking in the tavernas, concerts and various other events. On the next Saturday, the float of the Queen of the Carnival appears, escorted by the heralds of King Carnival. The greatest frolic follows the next day (Sunday). At noon the famous chocolate battle is fought, and in the afternoon, the great Carnival parade takes place, with scores of floats and thousands of merrymakers in fancy dress. In the evening there is another parade, with illuminated floats, culminating at 10 p.m. with the burning of

King Carnival in the main square of the town amid scenes of lively enthusiasm. The rest of the night is spent in song and dance. There are, needless to say, firework displays and masquerades galore, and open-air dancing in the Municipal Theatre square, where there is space for 2,000 dancers.

Naoussa (Macedonia), Castoria (Macedonia) and other provincial towns also offer Carnival festivities.

CULTURAL

Outstanding is the **Epidaurus Festival*** held in the ancient theatre of Epidaurus (about 120 miles from Athens), which apart from its superb setting possesses also excellent acoustics. Each year, during the latter half of June and the first half of July, ancient Greek tragedies and comedies are performed by the Greek National Theatre company.

The **Athens Festival** is held during August and September in the romantic setting of the Herod Atticus open-air ancient theatre at the foot of the Acropolis. Concerts, opera and ballet are featured, and world-famous conductors and soloists participate in the Athens State Orchestra concerts. Ancient Greek tragedies and comedies are also performed by the Greek National Theatre.

NATIONAL OR SPECIAL DAYS

March 25th is **Independence Day,** commemorating the day in 1821 when the Greeks gained their freedom from Turkish rule. There are military parades in Athens.

Also to be noted are October 26th (**Liberation Day**), with parades in Salonika, and October 28th (the Day when Greece entered the Second World War).

Other special days are the **Sponge Divers' Festival** and the original **" Dwarfs' Festival "** at Rhodes; an **Embroidery Exhibition** at Salonika; while **Classical Music concerts** are held on the island of Mytilene, as well as an **Anemone Festival** and fishing contests.

EASTER CELEBRATIONS

This holiday is the most important festivity of the Greek nation, and is attended piously by the whole Greek population, with a series of picturesque religious ceremonies and rites. The celebrations begin on Palm Sunday and continue until Easter Monday. The ceremonies of Good Friday, Holy Saturday and Easter Day always have particular pomp. Funeral services are held on Good Friday in all Greek churches; in the evening of the same day, the Epitaph Procession is held through the streets of all towns and villages, followed by thousands of persons holding dark-coloured or draped candles. The impressive Resurrection Mass is sung on the night of Holy Saturday, and at midnight, the clergy, accompanied by the choir, leave the churches to chant the Resurrection Hymn in the open. At that very moment, the stillness of the night is broken by joyful bell-ringing, whilst the worshippers light their candles, embrace each other with the " kiss of love " and take part in the rejoicing for the Resurrection, which includes fireworks, the detonation of petards, etc. Easter Day is an all-day celebration, with heavy eating and drinking, dancing and singing.

Easter celebrations are particularly picturesque in the countryside, especially in the mountain villages. On the nights of Good Friday and Holy Saturday, the mountain passes and the narrow streets of the Greek villages give the illusion of having been decorated with thousands of minute stars, which are really the flames of candles. Vast quantities of mutton and lamb are roasted on spits on Easter Day, and during the celebrations there are typical Greek national dances. Visitors, by the way, are welcome as guests at all Greek houses.

Hundreds of excursions are organised from Athens to villages in the surrounding countryside. Livadhia and Arachova are two suggestions for their popular rejoicings. Celebrations in Greek military barracks are also picturesque, particularly in the Athens area. Tons of " ovelias " (roasted sheep) are cooked in the barracks, and it is customary for visits to be paid by the King, members of the Royal Family, the Prime Minister and other high-ranking officials, who knock their Easter eggs with those of the soldiers. Especially brilliant are the celebrations in the barracks of the Royal Guard of Athens, where the Evzones (kilted soldiers) and knickerbocker-wearing Cretans dance with particular zest and provide excellent opportunities for photographers.

Corfu, Easter Eve Litany. This is the oldest litany on the island, instituted in 1553 after St. Spyridon, the island's patron saint, saved Corfu by miracle from a famine due to crop-failure.

Megara (10 miles from Athens), National folk dances in traditional costumes, Easter Tuesday.

OTHER RELIGIOUS AND TRADITIONAL EVENTS

Epiphany Feast and Consecration of the waters, Piraeus and all cities and towns by the sea, January 6th.

Thebes, Celebration of the **" Vlach Wedding,"** first day of Lent. An amusing parody of a Vlach (a characteristic highland people) wedding.

Messolonghi, April 26th. A celebration in commemoration of the sortie of Messolonghi (associations with Byron) in 1826.

Arachova, May 4th. In this picturesque village on the way to Delphi, which is known for its loom industry, there is a traditional running contest and dance by old men, young adults and children.

Macrynitsa (Pilion), May feast, May 2nd-4th. A festival consecrated to the pagan Spring.

Menidi, early May. A fair and colourful dances in local costume.

Edessa (Macedonia), Festival of Flowers, May. This festival includes parades of flower-covered floats, girls dressed in traditional costumes, and other artistic activities.

Langadas and **Ayi Eleni** (reached from Salonika), " Anastesaria " Feast, May 21st. Celebrated in accordance with traditional pagan and Byzantine rites, this festival includes the spectacle of the townsfolk who walk barefooted on burning embers.

Athens, " Sound and Light," Acropolis,* May-September. In the setting of the Sacred Rock of the Acropolis, the spectators on the Pynx may watch the alternating lighting of the monuments while listening to the transmission of recorded historical texts (given on different occasions in Greek, French, English and German) accompanied by music and sound effects. This is, in my opinion, one of the most fascinating after-dark entertainments in Europe.

There is also a " Sound and Light " spectacle at the Castle of the Grand Master of the Knights of Jerusalem in **Rhodes** (May-September); the subject is the conquest of Rhodes by Soliman the Magnificent.

Piraeus, Navy Week, June. In commemoration of those who have brought glory to Greece and distinguished themselves on the high seas. Activities include sea-sports and contests, parades, fleet exercises, etc.

Piraeus, Dora Stratou Folk Dance Group, June to September. This group offers outstanding performances of folk dances in national costumes at the ancient theatre, Philhelhinon Street.

Ponticonissi (Corfu), Festival and Fair, August 6th. This is a religious celebration on the beautiful wooded islet off the Corfu coast. The Corfiotes going to Ponticonissi in hundreds of little boats offer a picturesque sight.

Corfu, Celebration in honour of St. Spyridon, August 11th. There are religious processions and colourful folk festivities. The Church of St. Spiridon shelters under its roof the sacred relic of the Saint, brought from Constantinople in 1456.

Tinos (Cyclades), Pilgrimage, August 15th. Thousands of Greek Orthodox pilgrims visit the island on this day to pay homage at the miraculous ikon of the Holy Virgin. There are religious processions of great interest.

Zakynthos, August 20th-25th. Commemoration of St. Dionyssios, patron saint of the island. Processions and picturesque folklore festivities.

Salonika, St. Demetrius' Day (October 26th). Celebrating the city's patron saint, there are impressive religious processions and services at the famous Byzantine basilica of St. Demetrius. There is also a National Day, an official parade before the King on October 28th, the anniversary of the date on which Greece entered the Second World War.

SPORTING FIXTURES

At Athens, in late May, there is the **Acropolis Rally,** which is part of the international tourist championship. There are **yachting regattas** at Piraeus and elsewhere. **International tennis championships** are usually held at Athens in the early autumn, including competitions for the Eastern Mediterranean Challenge Cup.

WINE FESTIVAL

Each year at Daphni (near Athens) a **Wine Festival** is held, during September-October, in the park of the famous Byzantine Daphni Monastery. The best wines from all parts of Greece are displayed and visitors can drink at will without charge. Meals are served in a special taverna. During weekdays, artistic performances are given, such as folklore dancing, while distinguished Greek actors also take part in these manifestations. There is also a **Vintage Festival** at Rhodes.

CHAPTER THIRTEEN

Holland

THE MENTION OF HOLLAND IMMEDIATELY CONJURES UP IN MY mind the riotous colour of the bulb fields in spring, best seen around mid-April to mid-May between Leiden and Haarlem and in the Alkmaar region in the north. It is not surprising, then, that flowers play a major part in the festivities of her people. Amongst the many events, the " Keukenhof " National Flower Show at Lisse is outstanding and certainly the best known.

Tradition, too, has retained a firm place in the life of the people of Holland. You can see it in the costumes still worn in some villages and towns, and in the colourful markets of which the traditional Cheese Market at Alkmaar has earned the widest reputation. Culturally, the Holland Festival from mid-June to mid-July offers a fine programme of concerts, opera and ballet, especially in Amsterdam and Scheveningen.

AGRICULTURAL, HORTICULTURAL AND LIVESTOCK SHOWS

Flower Auction, Aalsmeer, every morning. Aalsmeer's large auction hall is alive with colour and activity as commercially grown flowers change hands and leave for the markets of the world. Many cases of them are sent immediately by air from Amsterdam's Schipol Airport.

Flora Flower Show, Heemstede, end of March to May every ten years.

National Flower Show " Keukenhof," * Lisse, end of March to May. The best known of Holland's many superb flower shows. During this period, similar events well worth seeing, though on a smaller scale, are held at Bennebroek (Linnaeushof Flower Show) and Hillegom (Treslong Flower demonstration gardens). During the second half of April, lovely flower mosaics can be seen at Limmen.

CARNIVALS

An outstanding **Carnival** is the three-day affair held each March at Maastricht. Similar gay events take place at the same time at Nijmegen and in the province of Brabant.

Flower Procession, Sassenheim-Lisse-Hillegom and return, Saturday during second half of April. Perhaps the finest of the many which take place in Holland. Floral floats proceed along a ten-mile route.

Flower Festivals, between mid-July and mid-September, mostly in western Holland in the area from The Hague to Haarlem. Nearly every year towns such as Leiden, Rotterdam, Haarlem, Aalsmeer hold flower processions and elect a flower queen. The event is usually accompanied by a programme of entertainments. The annual **Aalsmeer Flower Parade and Procession,** from Aalsmeer to the Olympic Stadium in Amsterdam takes place early in September; on the preceding day there is a public inspection of the floats in the Aalsmeer Auction Halls.

CULTURAL EVENTS

St. Matthew Passion, Naarden, end of March or early April. Several performances of Bach's great work, held in the church ; also performances in the Concertgebouw at Amsterdam.

Holland Festival, in most towns but principally in Amsterdam, The Hague, Scheveningen and Rotterdam, mid-June to mid-July. A month of music, opera and ballet, with a special opportunity of hearing little known works. There is also an **International Film Week.**

Sound and Light Performances, July to September. The most outstanding are held in front of the Knights' Hall in The Hague and in the picturesque little town of Wijk bij Duurstede in Utrecht province. There is every likelihood, too, that the excellent performances staged since 1960 in the restored historic Abbey of Middelburg will be repeated in future years.

Also to be noted is the **International Contest for Organists** on the famous organ of St. Bavo's Cathedral, Haarlem—in July. In contrast there is the **Blokker Festival of Light Music,** with the world's top-jazz and light orchestras competing, at Blokker (near Hoorn) in early May.

NATIONAL OR SPECIAL DAYS

H.M. Queen Juliana's Birthday, April 30th. On this national holiday, the Queen makes a personal appearance at her Soestidijk Palace home, not far from Hilversum. Many children wear orange ribbons in their hair to salute the House of Orange, and there are private parties and special attractions all over the country.

National Day, May 5th. A national holiday, with military parades in most cities, special concerts, and a Commemoration Service held on the Dam Square in Amsterdam.

Arnhem, Airborne Operations Day. In memory of the Battle of Arnhem, September 17th.

RELIGIOUS EVENTS

Passion Play, Tegelen, end of May to early September every five years. About 500 villagers take part in this beautiful biblical pageant, staged in a splendid open air theatre. It was last performed in 1960.

Similar performances, though on a smaller scale, take place every few years at Hertme, between Almelo and Hengelo in eastern Holland.

Famous is the **Silent Procession** in Amsterdam (March 4th). This commemorates the Holy Miracle of Amsterdam in the 15th century, and it takes place after dark. Although processions are against the law, this one with over 30,000 Roman Catholic men and boys is permitted.

SPORTING FIXTURES

Eleven Towns Tour, Friesland, at irregular intervals early in the year, subject to ice conditions. A 120-mile marathon on ice skates along the frozen canals, rivers and lakes. Regrettably, during recent years the weather has rarely been cold enough to make the event possible.

International Tulip Rally Races, Zandvoort Circuit, near Haarlem, April or May. Holland's biggest international motor rally.

Netherlands Grand Prix Motor Car Races, Zandvoort Circuit, near Haarlem, May or June. The biggest motor racing event of the year in Holland (valid for World Championships).

International TT Races Netherlands Grand Prix, Drent Circuit, Assen, during summer (valid for World Championships).

International Four Days Long-distance Marches, Nijmegen, end of July. About 5,000 competitors, including members of London's Metropolitan Police, take part in this *wandel mars* or walking march, a test of endurance and technique. Groups are divided into various categories: men only, ladies only, mixed, children, and everyone enters with great zeal into the daily marches of 20-30 miles which radiate from Nijmegen. Prizes are awarded, not for speed, but for unfaltering pace and group technique.

Kaagweek, Kaag Lake, near Leiden, end of July. Big yachting regattas, one of the three main sailing events.

Holland Week, Loosdrecht Lakes, near Hilversum, early August. International yachting competitions.

Sneekweek, Sneek Lake, near Leeuwarden, mid-August. Big yachting regattas, one of the three main sailing events.

Other sporting fixtures include the **Netherlands Skutsjesilen,** a regatta for old-type barges still in commercial use, at Sneek or vicinity, early August, and the **International Rally** of " Federation of Veteran Car Clubs," Amsterdam-Utrecht-Zandvoort, early October.

TRADE FAIRS

International Trade Fair, Utrecht. Held twice a year, in March and September; this is the biggest event of its kind in Holland.

Ancient Art and Antiques Fair, Prinsenhof Museum, Delft, end of August to early September.

International Radio Show, Amsterdam, early September.

London, England   *Ceremony of the Keys*

Olney, England   *Pancake Race*

Aalsmeer, Holland   *Flower Auction*

Epidaurus, Greece   *Festival Play*

TRADITIONAL CUSTOMS

Easter Customs, particularly in Gelderland and Twenthe. Bonfires glow round the ponds of the Hoge Veluwe National Park, near Arnhem, and across the countryside of Twenthe in eastern Holland. In Twenthe the *vloggelen* and Easter log-pulling are especially attractive. *Vloggelen* takes place in Ootmarsum in the province of Overijssel, when a long " crocodile " of people winds through the streets of the old town singing the centuries-old Easter song. Nearby, Denekamp is well known for its Easter log-pulling. The tree is felled and dragged to a meadow by a " crocodile " of people.

Cheese Market,* Alkmaar, every Friday from early May to September. A special train known as the Cheese Express runs from Rotterdam/The Hague and another from Amsterdam to this picturesque market which has been going on in the same way for centuries. Porters in traditional Guild costume carry the round yellow cheeses on special biers to the scales, where the Master of the Scales impassively notes down the results. Buying and selling follows a curious procedure in which one of the bargainers slaps the hand of the other as offers are accepted or rejected. All these transactions are settled by word of mouth.

Cheese Market, Gouda, every Thursday from May to October. Not as picturesque as the one at Alkmaar, but well worth a visit. You can see, too, a film showing how Gouda cheese is made on the local farms.

Whitsun Customs. These vary in different parts of the country. In some, the " Whitsun Bride " makes her appearance, while in others there's dancing round the Maypole. Perhaps the most unusual custom is the celebration of " Lazybones," the dying winter-devil who must be driven out or conquered by ridicule. The tradition is followed in varying forms in many parts of the country, including Amsterdam. In places a straw effigy is thrown into the water and warm dough-balls with butter and treacle are eaten as soon as the baker sounds a horn announcing they are ready. Youngsters especially delight in waking late sleepers on this occasion, and " Lazybones " may well find old rubbish fastened to their doors. In Haarlem, there's a " Lazybones " market.

Schager Market, Schagen, every Thursday in July and August. Farmers and their wives in traditional costume drive their carriages into town from the surrounding countryside and turn market day into a folkloric event. This most attractive weekly occasion is accompanied by folk dancing in the open air.

Review of the Herring Fleet, Scheveningen, mid-May. The whole town turns out on this Flag Day to give the men a grand send-off as the fishing fleet puts out to sea on the first day of the herring season. Ships in harbour and fishing boats are aflutter with gay decorations.

'T Keatsen (ball game—forerunner of cricket), Friesland, first Wednesday in August. Try and witness the " P.C.-Partij " match of this

G

age-old ball game, for it's one of the greatest sporting events of the year when everyone takes a holiday.

Tilting at the Ring, mostly on the isle of Walcheren. Revived annually at various places, the most outstanding event for this medieval sport is held on the fourth Thursday in August at Middelburg, main town of the region, when hundreds of farmers in traditional costume spur their work horses towards targets suspended between two poles.

Tattoo by Dutch Forces, Market Square, Delft, end of August to early September.

Prinsjesdag, The Hague, third Tuesday in September. H.M. Queen Juliana drives through the streets in a golden coach to open the new session of the Netherlands Government.

Liberation of Leiden, Leiden, October 3rd. A procession of Spanish and Dutch forces in historical costume marks the anniversary of the lifting of the terrible Spanish siege in 1574. Traditional dish of the day consists of mashed potatoes, carrots, onions and boiled beef—the first food to be eaten in the starving city after the liberation.

Sinterklaas (St. Nicholas) Customs. This benevolent gentleman (ancestor of Santa Claus) will be found in the streets of every town, but he makes his major appearance in Amsterdam on the Saturday preceding December 6th. Appropriately for such a sea-girt land, he makes his arrival by boat to be met by a white horse which he then rides through the streets, accompanied by his faithful servant, Black Peter, and a big parade. Traffic stops and the children stare in awe. This is their day, but the grown-ups love it, too.

In the name of Sinterklaas stranger things yet happen on the Frisian Islands where, for one evening at least, the men assert their authority. Draped in white sheets, they scour the islands for any womenfolk who have dared venture out of doors after five o'clock. Up to midnight, woe betide any unfortunate found—for it means a ducking in the nearest pond!

Local Custom. A strange one in the village of Staphorst in eastern Holland concerns the presence of a special small window in each house, opening into the bedroom of the unmarried daughter of the family. On three evenings a week, this window is left open and the girl's lover climbs in after dark. Should a baby result, then a marriage is necessarily arranged. Oddly enough, Staphorst is a village which keeps itself to itself and is very severe otherwise in its religion and morals.

CHAPTER FOURTEEN

Iceland

PERHAPS ICELAND'S NUMEROUS GLACIERS HAVE EARNED HER this rather inhospitable name. Icelanders must often regret the misnomer, for their summers bear comparison with the best of Britain's and, during long midsummer days, her mountains stand bathed in the midnight sun.

While Iceland's sparse population is centred in highly modern townships and she can boast the oldest existing parliament in the world, this is essentially a land for nature lovers who like wild, untrammelled countryside, rare plants and birds, and such extravagances of nature as hot springs and volcanoes right up by the Arctic Circle. Of her annual events, the Westman Islands Celebration early in August is a gay and unsophisticated occasion in glorious surroundings, while the sheep round-ups in late August or early September present perhaps the best opportunity to join Icelanders in festivities which are an essential part of their way of life.

NATIONAL OR SPECIAL DAYS

Children's Day, all over the country, April 24th. The first day of summer, according to the old Icelandic calendar, is now devoted to the youngsters, with a children's parade and amusements in cinemas and assembly halls.

Sailors' Day, first Sunday in June. A day for rowing and swimming competitions, speeches and dances.

National Day, all over the country, June 17th. This is the more important of Iceland's two national days and celebrates the proclamation of the Republic in 1944. It is also the birthday of Jon Sigurdsson, often named the father of free Iceland. A varied programme of parades, sporting competitions, outdoor concerts and shows, speeches and amusements culminates in the evening with dancing in the streets of Reykjavik and other towns and villages into the early hours of the morning.

National Day, all over the country, December 1st. It was on this day in 1918 that Iceland gained her independence, though remaining under the Danish crown. It is now largely a student celebration.

New Year's Eve, all over the country, but mainly in Reykjavik, December 31st. At midnight, all ships in harbour sound their pipes and a big firework display bursts against the dark winter sky. Dancing in all restaurants.

SPORTING FIXTURES

Fishing Festival, Westman Islands, early June. An international fishing event, about seven miles off the southern coast of Iceland. The festival, centred at the islands' main fishing village, lasts three days.

TRADITIONAL CUSTOMS

Thorrablót, Reykjavik, late January and early February. A gastronomic occasion during which some of the city's restaurants serve traditional Icelandic food. This includes heavily smoked mutton, brisket of lamb preserved in sour whey, singed heads of lamb, shark, and various kinds of sausages made of liver, blood and loins of lamb and preserved in sour whey.

Westman Islands Celebration, first week-end in August. The small valley of Herjólfsdalur is the scene of the festivities which begin on the Friday afternoon. The weekend's programme includes sporting events, outdoor concerts and variety shows, dancing, but the highlight is on the second day, when a young man swings on a rope from the top of a crag rising from the floor of the valley. For centuries, this method has been used for gathering sea-fowl eggs from the cliffs. During the celebrations, nearly every family in the Westman Islands, and a good many visitors too, camp in Herjólfsdalur.

Sheep Round-Ups, all over the country, end of August or early September. There are four sheep for every inhabitant of Iceland, so round-up time is quite an impressive event. Flocks are gathered from the mountain pastures and driven into folds in each county. Here, the animals are separated by their owners, providing at the same time an occasion for celebration and, afterwards, dancing in the county assembly halls.

CHAPTER FIFTEEN

Ireland

THE GREAT CHARM OF IRELAND, AS FAR AS I AM CONCERNED,
lies in the unspoilt nature of her countryside and the friendly exuberance
of her people which guarantees a welcome to strangers wherever or
whenever they may go. The exuberance finds an outlet in the Irish love
of sport, particularly if there's an element of gambling attached to it.
Because they also breed some of the finest horses in the world, it is hardly
surprising that the Irish Racing Calendar is the fullest in Europe, headed
by the Irish Derby in June. Horses and horsemanship *par excellence* also
account for the year's most fashionable event, the Royal Dublin Society's
Horse Show in August.

But if Ireland is known the world over for her racing stock, she has
also made a name for her contributions to the arts. Of the many annual
cultural festivals, the Wexford Festival of Music and the Arts is the most
important and the most unusual.

AGRICULTURAL, HORTICULTURAL AND LIVESTOCK SHOWS

Royal Dublin Society's Spring Show and Industries Fair,
Ballsbridge, early May. This " shop window " of Irish agriculture and
industry includes all types of farm livestock of prize winning quality.
Horse jumping events are arranged for each day of the show.

Royal Dublin Society's Horse Show,* Ballsbridge, August. A
very fashionable event which attracts up to 120,000 visitors from all parts
of the world and includes outstanding horse jumping events, an industrial
display and flower show. Be warned that Dublin's hotels get extremely
crowded at this time.

Puck Fair and Pattern, Killorglin, Co. Kerry, for three days,
usually in the first half of August. The three days are known respectively
as " Gathering Day," " Puck Fair Day " and " Scattering Day." On the
first evening, a large puck goat in a spacious cage is ceremoniously
carried, amidst much merriment, to a raised platform in the square at the
centre of the town. Here, King Puck remains enthroned to preside over
the events of the next two days—a great cattle, sheep and horse fair, and
crowds engaged in commerce and amusement. On the third evening, Puck
leaves his throne to be borne triumphantly back through the streets.

95

Stock Shows occur around the country all through the year. Many of them are well worth visiting for their lively atmosphere—and a sight of the high quality livestock for which Ireland is famous.

National Ploughing Championships, held at a different place each year, in the autumn. Contestants come from as far as Canada to compete in this event.

CULTURAL EVENTS

International Festival of Music and The Arts, Dublin, a week in June.

Dublin Theatre Festival, Dublin, September. For two weeks productions of outstanding merit from Ireland and abroad are shown. Celebrity performances are always a feature.

Light Opera Festival, Waterford, September.

Wexford Festival of Music and The Arts, Wexford, end of September to early October. Though the festival offers a fine programme of music, opera, film shows, exhibitions and lectures, the stress is on Italian opera and particularly on those lesser known. Wexford citizens are proud of their cultural tradition, and there's every chance that your taxi driver will give you an accurate rendering of excerpts from operas you may never have heard before !

International Film Festival, Cork, end of September to early October.

An Toireachtas, Dublin, a week in October. Ireland's premier Gaelic Cultural Festival of music, drama, literature, art, also includes Gaelic Games (hurling, football and handball).

NATIONAL OR SPECIAL DAYS

St. Patrick's Day, all over the country, March 17th. Especially notable in Dublin.

RELIGIOUS EVENTS

Pilgrimage to Knock, Co. Mayo, every Sunday from May to early October. The newest of Ireland's popular pilgrimages is attended by many invalids. The vision of Our Lady was seen at the little parish church of Knock on August 21st, 1879.

Pilgrimage to Station Island, Lough Derg, Co. Donegal, June to mid-August. Ireland's most important pilgrimage consists of three days of rigorous fasting on the island, also known as " St. Patrick's Purgatory " since, it is said, the saint spent 40 days of prayer and fasting there.

Pilgrimage to Croagh Patrick, Co. Mayo, last Sunday in July. Thousands of pilgrims, some of them barefooted, climb to the summit of Ireland's 2,510-foot Holy Mountain. A series of Masses are held in a little oratory on the mountain top.

SPORTING FIXTURES

Horse Racing. The Irish place horse racing above all else and there are, roughly speaking, about three events for every two days on the Irish Racing Calendar ! However, the most important are:

Irish Grand National, Fairyhouse, Co. Meath, early April.

Kildare and National Hunt, Punchestown, Co. Dublin, end of April.

Irish 2,000 Guineas and 1,000 Guineas, Curragh, Co. Kildare, May.

Irish Derby, Curragh, Co. Kildare, June. In 1962, the richest racing event in all Europe.

The " 1500," Phoenix Park, Dublin, August.

Irish St. Leger, Curragh, Co. Kildare, September.

Irish Cambridgeshire, Curragh, Co. Kildare, October.

Greyhound Racing. There are approximately 18 Greyhound Racing Tracks in Ireland, where meetings take place each evening during the period February 1st to November 30th. The National Coursing Clubs' Fixtures open in September and finish in March of the following year. The two principal meetings are:

National Meeting, Powerstown Park, Clonmel, early February.

Irish Cup Meeting, Clounanna, near Adare, end of February.

Sea Angling. The most important of the many events takes place at Westport, Co. Mayo, for a fortnight in June. Others are at: Wicklow, end of May; Slade, Co. Wexford, July; Moville, Co. Donegal, a week in August; Dingle, Co. Kerry, early September; Valentia Harbour, Co. Kerry, mid-September.

Hurling. Of the three Gaelic games played in Ireland—hurling, football and handball—hurling is the most popular and many matches take place from early spring through to Christmas. Played with camáns or hurleys (hip-high lengths of ash which have a broad base), it is the fastest field game in the world, and the small leather-covered ball travels at such speed that it is sometimes difficult for spectators to follow its flight. The All-Ireland Finals take place in September at Croke Park, Dublin.

TRADITIONAL CUSTOMS

Oyster Festival, Clarenbridge, Co. Galway, early September. The Mayor of Galway in scarlet robes opens and eats the first bivalve of the season on Clarenbridge pier. At Paddy Burke's pub, they serve oysters by the bucketful, to be liberally washed down with Guinness.

CHAPTER SIXTEEN

Italy

IN VIEW OF HER LENGTHY HISTORY ITALY POSSESSES A LARGE number of traditional festivals; and due to the enthusiasm of the people, the spectacular side of many manifestations commemorating special occasions, deeds and legends has become increasingly accentuated. Then, as one might expect, the musical side is an important factor at many celebrations.

Nearly every town and village has its own saint's day celebrations, but it is quite impossible to list them all here; yet most of them offer their own special features, while they offer the tourist a good opportunity to study the Italian character. Each year the Italian State Tourist Office issues a " Calendar of Events," but it is worth while also to get further lists from any places you intend visiting. I think you will find a great variety and richness in Italian folklore.

AGRICULTURAL, LIVESTOCK AND HORTICULTURAL SHOWS

At Verona in March there is a seven-day **Cattle and Agriculture Fair** which is an event of European renown. Over 6,000 horses are sold there yearly, while exhibits include everything that agriculture produces or requires.

San Remo has its **Flower Corso** in February, and Ventimiglia its **Battle of Flowers** in June. Palermo, too, has its **Festival of the Flowers** in late May and early June, with considerable cash prizes for the best exhibits. In Florence the Tuscan Horticultural Society stages early in May a fine **Display of Spring Flowers.**

Also very important is the **International Exhibition of Food Preserves and Packing Technique and International Industrial and Technical Salon of Food Equipment** held in Parma, during late September.

CARNIVALS

Carnival of Viareggio. The most important carnival in Italy, this begins in January and reaches its climax on Shrove Tuesday. Phantasmagorical processions depicting allegorical subjects in the most lively and expressive, shrewd and bizarre way, historical masks created with acute satire and parody, parades of festoons and flowers, sequences of lights and colours, a frenzy of dancing, the noise of trumpets, a confusion of confetti, the hectic merriment of the crowd, whether in masks or not, all take place in the brilliant setting of Viareggio. The figures and the set scenes on the floats have reached great artistry and are the work of specialised local craftsmen; they model their inventions of fancy in *papier mâché* and clay. These are mounted on gigantic floats to parade in the " Procession of Masks " known the world over. Interesting and original social, folklore and sporting events also take place in Viareggio during the Carnival, which vies with those of Nice, Basle, and Düsseldorf in attractiveness.

Smaller celebrations take place in various other towns, usually in the weeks preceding Lent including Bologna (Children's Carnival), Cuneo (Folklore and a rally for Piedmontese and Ligurian masks), Follonica (Grosseto), Ivrea Historic Carnival, celebrating the liberation of the city from the tyranny of a feudal lord. Some people wear costumes of Napoleonic times, and on the last few days there is the Battle of the Oranges. Other celebrations at this time are at San Remo (Battle of Flowers), Turin, Verona (the festival culminates in the distribution of " gnocchi " in the Square of the Basilica of San Zeno), Ascoli Piceno, etc.

Flower Festivals. In Italy—the land of flowers—there are many flower festivals that bring a special and incomparable note of beauty, poetry, grace and elegance to the full calendar of civil and religious festivals, palios and jousts, gastronomic fairs and art exhibitions.

Some of the flower festivals are famous and every year attract crowds, such as the splendid **Battle of Flowers** at Ventimiglia held in June, and the **Procession of Flowers** at Salsomaggiore (Parma) on the first Sunday in June.

Other flower festivals take place at San Remo, Alassio, Santa Margherita Ligure, Brunate and Tremezzo on Lake Como, Viggiu (Varese), Bolzano, Sorrento, Bari and Palermo.

CULTURAL EVENTS

The **Grand Opera Season** in Italy usually begins in December or January and continues through to April or May. The principal opera houses in Italy are La Scala in Milan, Teatro dell 'Opera in Rome, San Carlo in Naples and the Fenice in Venice. Operas are also performed in many other Italian towns during this period, such as in Florence at the Teatro Comunale, in Genoa at the Teatro Comunale dell 'Opera, in Parma at the Teatro Regio and in Palermo at the Teatro Massimo, to mention but a few.

During the summer there are open-air opera performances, the principal venues being those at the Arena of Verona* (mid-July to mid-

August) which enjoys perfect acoustics; the Terme di Caracalla in Rome (July-August) and the Arena Flegrea in Naples (July-August).

The two chief **Music Festivals** take place in Florence (Maggio Musicale Fiorentino) during May and June, and the International Music Festival at Venice in September.

Other musical festivals worth noting are:

Festival of Italian Song, San Remo, January.

International Jazz Music Festival, San Remo, March.

Music Festival, Assisi, April, with its Serenade of Calendimaggio— a musical contest between the two main quarters of the city.

Classical Dance Festival, Tremezzo Cadenabbia, May.

Wagnerian Music Festival, Ravello, June. Held in the delightful environment of the Gardens of the Villa Rufolo.

Summer Musical Festival, in the Arena Flegrea, Naples, July.

Open-Air Operetta Festival, San Giusto Castle, Trieste, July.

Opera, in the Lombardia Castle, Enna, during July.

International Poetry Prize, Capri, July.

International Poliphony Contest, Arezzo, August. This is one of the two contests of its kind in Europe.

International Piano Contest, Bolzano, August/September.

Opera Season, in the Roman Amphitheatre, Cagliari (Sardinia), August.

Autumn Festival of Operas and New Plays, Bergamo, September.

Siena Music Week, Siena, September.

Sagra Musicale Umbra, Perugia, last week in September.

Festival of the Two Worlds, Spoleto, July.

" G. B. Viotti " International Music Contest, Vercelli, October.

Worth noting, too, if you happen to be in Rome are the occasional open-air orchestral concerts given in the Basilica of Massentius, adjoining the Roman Forum. The setting is fascinating. For sacred music Rome is, of course, supreme. If you are interested, enquire at the Information Office about special choir services; High Mass on Sundays in St. Peter's can always be recommended.

Dramatic Performances may have a more limited appeal, but often the setting repays the visitor who is unable to understand Italian. Among these spectacles I would include the classical plays staged at Ostia Antica (easily reached from Rome) from June-July; in the celebrated Greek Theatre of Syracuse (June); in the Greek-Roman Theatre of Taormina; at Pompeii (with wonderful night illuminations); the Melodrama Festival in San Remo in February; and, not least, the traditional performances of classical plays given during September at Vicenza in the splendid setting designed by Andrea Palladio. Also of note are the " Sound and Light " spectacles (summer) at Hadrian's

Villa (Tivoli), the Forum in Rome, the " Magic Nocturne " at Frascati, and the illuminated fountain at Tivoli.

Sicily is famous for its **Marionette Theatres,** and although the performances are usually held in humble surroundings, yet it is interesting to attend a performance; Palermo is one of the best centres. The repertoire is based on episodes from the deeds of the Paladins, re-elaborated through the centuries by the puppetmasters to satisfy the taste of the public, who follow the events on the stage with child-like enthusiasm, and salute the appearance of the main characters with applause, shouts, howls and violent interjections according to their individual likes and dislikes. The most popular scenes are concerned with battles and duels; and the text of the play is a strange mixture of poetry and prose, poetic phrases distorted and dialect expressions.

The **International Ballet Festival** at Nervi during July is the only festival of its kind in Italy. It is held in the marvellous setting of the Teatro del Parco, every two years.

In September, Venice provides an **International Film Festival.** Founded in 1933, this is the oldest film festival in the world. The side events include some interesting retrospective shows. Rapallo holds each January an **International Show** of 8- and 16-millimetre films.

In the field of pictorial art, every other year sees the world famous **Biennale of Art** held in Venice from mid-June to mid-October (even years). Then, in Florence, there is invariably a special **Art Exhibition,** always worth a visit; and in La Spezia, there is a **National Painting Exhibition** every two years (odd years), for Italian and foreign artists alike.

Other occasional notable **Art Exhibitions** are in Rome, Milan, Naples, Turin, Vicenza, Bari, Volterra, and other major towns, while visitors to Rome should visit the Via Margutta—the artists' quarter—to see what's on.

A recent addition is the **International Salon for Humour,** at Bordighera in August.

RELIGIOUS EVENTS
January

Epiphany. Many beliefs and customs cluster about this ancient festival. A traditional figure called *La Befana*, a kindly but sharp-eyed old hag, awards, in her name, sweets for good children and lumps of coal for the naughty ones. I refer in a later section to the famous Fair in Rome at Piazza Navona, while in the Trastevere district of the city there is music and noise and puppet shows.

At **Piana Degli Albanesi** (Palermo), Epiphany is celebrated according to the Greek rite. The ceremony is completed by the " flight of the dove " and by a distribution of oranges. This is a wonderful opportunity of seeing the most beautiful costumes in Sicily.

At **Tarcento** (Udine), Epiphany is celebrated with interesting festivities, culminating in the evening in a torchlight procession which wends its way up a hill overlooking the town where a large glittering star has been lit. The costumes are of the 14th century.

Cividale del Friuli (Udine): in the Cathedrals the solemn rite of the **Mass of the Spadone** (broadsword) has been taking place for centuries on Epiphany. There is medieval music and Gregorian chants when the Deacon wears sumptuous robes, carries a plumed helmet, and salutes the faithful three times with the sword that dates back to 1366. Enormous crowds attend this ceremony.

Festival of St. Anthony Abbot, January 17th. He is the protector of domestic animals which are brought to the church to be blessed. In Rome this ceremony takes place in front of the Church of St. Eusebio where, in addition, little bread rolls are distributed to the faithful, for they are considered to have miraculous powers in curing animals.

Festival of St. Geminiano, Modena, January 31st. In honour of St. Geminiano (who saved the city from the scourge of Attila), the city fathers offer candles at the Cathedral preceded in procession by the town band and majordomos in 18th century costume. In the afternoon the traditional *tombola* is held, with fancy articles as prizes.

February

Feast of St. Agata, Catania, February 3rd-5th. The festival of the city's patron saint has a characteristic feature in the *Candelore*, curious wooden structures in the shape of bell-towers each about 20 ft. high, richly decorated and representing the various corporations. The *Candelore* follow the precious *Ferculo* of the saint, in which the relics are exposed for veneration. Participants in the procession through the streets of the city go barefoot; and during stops amidst the firing of muskets those carrying the *Candelore* compete against each other in the *annacata*; this is a dance in which each bearer waves his candle about to make it burn out first.

March

Procession of Holy Thursday, Caltanissetta (Sicily). Sixteen groups of statuary depicting the phases of Christ's Passion are carried in procession. The following day there is a solemn Procession of the Gentlemen of the City in which the craftsmen's guilds and the Clergy take part.

The Segavecchia, Forlimpopoli (Forli), Thursday in mid-Lent. A grotesque puppet depicting an old woman is carried through the streets of the town, accompanied by bands and allegorical floats.

April

Palm Sunday. This is the Sunday of peace, and olive branches, blessed by the priest, are still exchanged among relatives and friends, and kept the whole year through. In Rome, however, branches of palm (specially prepared to give them a golden tint) are sold in front of St. Peter's and given as gifts. These palms come from the Ligurian Riviera, and Bordighera, because of an historical event, has the privilege of providing the palms for the Roman basilicas.

The " Mysteries " of Holy Week. Noteworthy forms of popular dramatic art take place in many places in Italy during Holy Week. There are processions and sacred plays (also called " Mysteries ").

Among the most famous are the " Mysteries " at Trapani (Sicily), when enormous crowds gather to follow the procession of the 20 sacred groups, carried shoulder high, with intense emotion. Similar events take place all over Sicily. The procession of the " Mysteries " at Taranto is of ancient origin. Participants wear similar vestments to those seen in Seville. Eight groups of *papier mâché* statues, of exquisite workmanship, are used in the procession.

The **Good Friday Procession** at Frassinoro (Modena) is a living presentation of the " Via Crucis." In the houses of the town the tradition of depicting this or that sacred personage is handed down from father to son, either preserving or renewing the suitable costumes. Groups of families join together to vie with one another in organising a " living tableau " of the Passion. This night-procession proceeds through the town and on the slopes of the surrounding mountains by the light of torches.

Procession of the Dead Christ, Grassina (Florence), Good Friday. An interesting ceremony at night during which the Passion of Christ is recalled; 1,000 characters take part.

At Barile (Potenza) there is a **Good Friday Procession** in which the various stages of the Crucifixion are presented by living actors. The Mass is also interesting because it is based upon the Greek-Orthodox liturgy which was used until some time ago, for the population is of Albanian origin.

Savona has the traditional and impressive **Good Friday Procession** of the prized 18th century *Casse*, which are the work of distinguished sculptors.

Sulmona's **Good Friday Procession** features what is known as the *Tronco*, a large, empty cross lined with crimson velvet and trimmed with silver. It was constructed in 1750.

Every inhabitant of Sezze Romano (Latina), without exception, takes part in performances of dramatic episodes from the **Great Passion Play*** during Holy Week. The historical tradition of the sequence of the episodes in the drama is rigidly adhered to, with scenes from both the Old and New Testaments. The auditorium is a natural amphitheatre seating 100,000 spectators, and the drama is repeated during the summer, thus offering a profoundly moving spectacle of high dramatic value.

Easter Celebrations at Piana Degli Albanesi (Palermo) are according to the Byzantine rite. On this occasion, too, the women wear the characteristic oriental costumes. The ceremony of the distribution and benediction of the red eggs is singular.

May

Festival of San Nicola,* Bari. The patron saint of this great city is commemorated in May when a large number of festivities take place in honour of the removal of the bones in 1087 from the orient. Apart from the processions, with historical groups, the battle of flowers, the fireworks, etc., the singular thing about this event is the ceremony on the sea. The statue of the Saint is taken from the Basilica and carried amongst a huge crowd of the faithful (numerous pilgrims come from neighbouring towns and villages to fulfil vows or to implore grace) to the quay from which it is transported on a decorated boat to a neighbouring beach followed by innumerable craft carrying groups of the faithful.

Many pilgrims who come to the Festival of San Nicola (Our Santa Claus) take advantage of the proximity of two other famous shrines in Apulia: the shrine of San Michele in the ancient town of Monte Sant' Angelo, and the Sanctuary della Madonna dell'Incoronata, both near to Foggia.

The **Festival of San Michele** takes place at Monte Sant'Angelo from May 1st to 10th. The little town is magnificently situated on a spur of Monte Gargano, and the sanctuary lies in a grotto said to have been consecrated by the Saint in 490. A long stairway leads down to this cave which has at its entrance a fine bronze Byzantine door. Inside, the pilgrims become most emotional, weeping, sobbing and imploring the Saint for his help. They crowd to kiss his statue or to touch it with a handkerchief which is afterwards preserved as a relic. The heat that comes from many bodies and the lights of a thousand candles is intense. After their devotions the pilgrims come out to the open air to make merry. This, in fact, is a most typical South Italian festival. Not far away, incidentally, is the bleak village of San Giovanni Rotondo, famous for its living saint, Padre Pio. He is a truly wonderful man and bears on his hands, feet and side the visible stigmata, like St. Francis, which have bled every day since 1918.

Festival at the Sanctuary of the Crowned Virgin from the last Saturday of April to June 13th. There is an interesting legend about the origin of this holy place, which lies in the woods of Alberona and dates back to the early 11th century. A temporary village comes into being for the annual festival. On arrival the pilgrims make three circuits of the sanctuary, singing and praying. The first day they are accompanied by a " Cavalcade of Angels "—young boys dressed in white, holding the sword of the Archangel and riding elegantly covered horses. After their devotions to the Madonna, the pilgrims enjoy themselves, eating, drinking, playing and singing in the woods. This festival is linked with that at Monte Sant'Angelo.

Feast of Sant'Efisio, * Cagliari. This is one of the most picturesque processions in the world due to the magnificent costumes. At 11 a.m. on May 1st the image of the Saint is carried with great pomp on a coach to the church of Pula where he suffered martyrdom. Here the faithful eat a rich meal exceeding ten dishes. On the 4th the image with a mounted escort returns to Cagliari. What makes this procession so spectacular are the picturesque costumes worn by those in the procession, most of them peasants, the ribbon and flower decorations of the coach drawn by pairs of oxen, and the characteristic sound of the " launeddas."

Festival of the Mysteries, Campobasso. Living groups depict scenes from the Old and New Testaments and are carried in procession. It has been held since 1749.

Wedding of the Sea, Cervia (Ravenna). This is the benediction of the sea when the Bishop of Cervia symbolically throws a wedding ring into the water.

Festival of St. Dominic, Cocullo (L'Aquila). Held on the first Thursday in May, this is one of the most curious festivals in Italy. The statue of the Saint, wrapped in living snakes, is carried in procession through the streets. Peasants throw serpents on to the statue, shouting and singing with an exultation that is pagan. In fact, there is a distinct link between the cult of St. Dominic (who gives protection against bites of snakes, hydrophobia and even toothache) and the worship of the goddess Angizia, whose name was derived from the word *anguis* (snake).

A pagan origin can also be seen in the **Feast of San Zopito** which takes place annually at Loreto Aprutino (Pescara) on Pentecost Monday. This feast centres around a white and dignified ox which is led in procession into the church, its horns decorated with flowers and coloured ribbons. On its back there sits a boy with angelic wings, his head adorned with flowers, holding in his hands a parasol.

Mention might be made here of an unusual **Beauty Contest** held annually (August-September) in one or other of the towns of this region. For the prize is awarded not merely to a beautiful girl, wearing traditional costume, but to one who is also clever in domestic virtues, including an ability to cook, sew and embroider.

The "Infiorata," Genzano (Rome). On Corpus Christi day, a splendid and multicoloured carpet of flowers is laid along the Via Livia.

The Feast of the Ascension, Venice. Ever since its institution " La Festa della Sensa " has been the most solemn, the most magnificent, the most spectacular, the most impressive, and the most beautiful of the Venetian festivals. Its celebration is interwoven with the history of the Republic for seven centuries, down to our own day. To-day, however, it has not the importance and attraction it once held for the citizens of this lovely city.

The Miracle of San Gennaro,* Naples, first Saturday in May (also on September 19th). This Miracle, or the liquefaction of the blood of St. Januaris, takes place on these two dates. It was his aged nurse who collected some of the saint's blood at the time of his martyrdom in A.D. 305, and her descendants, known as the " relations of San Gennaro," are still entitled to a front place at the rite. The precious ampulla containing the blood is brought to the high altar of the Cathedral and placed before a silver statue of the saint which contains his skull. Above the prayers of the congregation, the organ and the chanting of the priest can be heard the invocation of the " relations." If the blood is slow to liquefy, the crowd massed in the piazza outside takes up the cry and even hurls insults at the patron. Suddenly, the blood liquefies and there are the wildest scenes of enthusiasm, while all the bells of the city toll in joy. San Gennaro has worked the miracle again. Each time the miracle is repeated for eight consecutive days.

Concurrently at Pozzuoli the miracle manifests itself on a stone stained with the blood of the Patron Saint.

June

Festival of the Carmine, Naples, June 16th. Naples is a very religious-minded city; this can be gauged at every turn from the infinite number of shrines of Saints to be seen on every corner, and from the devotion of its inhabitants. It would be an impossible task to mention each one, so all I can do is to stress that in every case the petards put in an appearance, the illuminations are switched on, and often little concerts are given on an improvised platform in the middle of alleys, drawing admiring crowds of girls and youths in the quarter. A notable festival is the Festival of the Madonna del Carmine, in the quarter of the same name. On this occasion, apart from the usual illuminations and fireworks, there is the conflagration of the Campanile—a mock fire prepared with such realism that it is astonishingly effective.

The **Festival of the Madonna dell' Arco** is another notable event in Naples, celebrated two days after Pentecost. It is a singular pilgrimage to this Sanctuary which is situated about six miles from the city. While many people go there by car, an unusual feature of this pilgrimage is that those who are making it for the purpose of keeping a vow, out of devotion, or to implore grace from the miraculous Madonna, must go there on foot without halting.

Feast of the Vow, Assisi, last Sunday in June. An historical and religious event in memory of a miracle performed by Santa Chiara in 1241.

Procession of St. Vito, Marano (Udine), June 15th. A colourful

Venice, Italy

Water Fête

Siena, Italy

Il Palio

Dublin, Ireland   *Horse Show*

Bari, Italy   *Festival of St. Nicholas*

religious event in the lagoon on the occasion of the festival of the patron saint, St. Vito. The figure of the Saint is taken out on a large raft, followed by a long procession of gaily decorated boats. Although this procession is a simple affair, it is a singularly picturesque spectacle.

Festival of San Giovanni, Isola Comacina (Como), June 25th-26th. Sacred procession of boats to the island, with illuminations and folklore events.

Festival of the " Palombella," Orvieto, Whitsun. This festival of the wood-pidgeon commemorates the descent of the Holy Spirit on the Apostles in the supper-room. Shortly afterwards there is the Feast of Corpus Christi in Orvieto. It is celebrated with a picturesque procession commemorating the introduction of the festival by Pope Urban IV in 1260.

Festival of the " Four Altars," Torre del Greco (Naples). A popular and religious festival in memory of the liberation of the city from medieval vassalage.

Miracle of the Corporal,* Orvieto, Corpus Christi. Against the marvellous background of the façade of Orvieto Cathedral there is performed an historical play commemorating the miracle of Bolsena, which resulted in the building of the cathedral. It happened that a Bohemian priest doubted the doctrine of the Real Presence of Our Lord in the Blessed Sacrament. Disturbed by his doubts he set out for Rome, but at Bolsena while celebrating a Mass he saw drops of red blood upon the Corporal. Thus was instituted the magnificent festival of Corpus Christi, for Pope Urban IV resolved that this was a true miracle.

July

Feast of Santa Rosalia, Palermo, mid-July. This is one of the most sumptuous and interesting events in Sicily. It originated in 1225 when Palermo was decimated by the plague. Then came the news that the bones of Saint Rosalia had been discovered on Mount Pellegrino where the virgin had withdrawn and where she had died. When the sacred relics were found and borne in solemn procession the plague died away. The festival is characterised by a colossal triumphal carriage.

Feast of the Redeemer, Venice, third Sunday in July. It dates back to the year when the people of Venice made a vow on the Giudecca Island for liberation from the plague. The date is still solemnised with great pomp and constitutes one of the most traditional celebrations in the city. On the embankment of the Zattere and the Giudecca there are special illuminations and fireworks which reflect on the waters with picturesque effects of colour. There is a procession at night across a bridge of boats. Then, amid songs and music of all kinds, the boats spread out over the canals of the city to assemble at the Lido later on, there to await the sunrise.

Harvest Festivals. Between June and July the crops in Italy are reaped. At this time there is the singing of religious songs, and it is considered blasphemous to sing love or humorous songs. In several villages the rites assume particular solemnity and have their own special characteristics. At Jelsi (Molise) there is the traditional "**Sagra del Grano**" which takes place on July 26th. On this occasion there is the interesting procession of the *Traglie*, a very ancient vehicle resembling a sleigh, each vehicle being elaborately ornamented and drawn by adorned pairs of pure white oxen. Alongside each *traglia* walk the women of Jelsi dressed in their rich traditional costumes. The procession continues for hours, and on all sides there is gaiety in this little-known region, which is so rich in beauty.

Another event which is rich in interest is the **Festa del Grano,** of an agricultural-religious character, which takes place at Agrigento on the first and second Sundays in July in honour of the patron saint of the town, Saint Calogero.

August

Festival of the Pardon, Assisi. A festival that commemorates August 2nd, 1216, when St. Francis obtained indulgence from Pope Honorius III.

Feast of the Redeemer,* Nuoro (Sardinia), end of August. Procession of the people, wearing traditional costumes, to the top of Monte Ortobene where the statue of the Redeemer is to be found. The event culminates in the " Festival of the Costume " in which groups compete, executing Sardinian dances and singing traditional songs, thus providing a spectacle that is unique of its kind.

Festival of the " Candelieri," Sassari, August 14th. The twelve *candelieri*, heavy wooden columns carved and embellished, are carried each on the shoulders of eight strong youths who execute the " dances " as they proceed along the route. Along the flanks are drummers and flute players and the important members of the *gremio* dressed in the ancient costumes that are Spanish in style.

September

Festival of Santa Rosa, Viterbo, September 3rd. This one-time medieval residence of the Popes has a festival that rather resembles that of Santa Rosalia at Palermo, for it is characterised by an imposing wooden " machine " (90 ft. high), with designs that vary from year to year. On ts summit stands the resplendent statue of the Saint. Lit with 1,500 candles, the structure is carried by 85 bearers called *facchini* who wear a red and white costume. The procession presents quite a fantastic sight as it wends its way through the city, the tower competing in height with the ancient buildings poised darkly against the star-studded sky.

Traditional Illuminations of Santa Croce, Lucca, mid-September. This is one of the oldest Catholic celebrations, when the famous " Holy Face," believed to have been carved out of cedar of Lebanon, is venerated.

The Miracle of San Gennaro, Naples, September 19th. For description see May.

November

Festival of the Madonna della Salute, Venice, November 21st. Religious celebrations to commemorate the end of the Plague of 1630, which resulted in the building of the Church of the same name.

December

Translation of the Holy House, Loreto, early December. For this festival great bonfires are lit during the night throughout the country-side of the Marches. Solemn religious celebrations take place in the Sanctuary itself and in the Square outside.

Feast of Santa Lucia, Syracuse, December 13th. It commemorates the martyrdom of a Saint who was killed on December 13th, 1304. This is almost a pagan festival, but then in Sicily the people take their religion with full emotion. Saint Lucy, with her eyes on a salver (as she is often depicted), as a subject for art, is both repulsive and unaesthetic; but her sufferings, like those of Saint Agatha, necessarily reflect in the imagination of her legend-weavers something of the morbid uncanniness of the land-scapes which surround her birthplace. Actually, there is no authentic reason for supposing that she was blinded in the horrible manner in which some modern hagiographers describe. It is, indeed, far pleasanter to think of gentle Lucy, " the enemy of all that cruel is," as Dante saw her in his poet's dream. Her lovely eyes, those eyes *belli, lucenti,* must have gazed over and over again upon those wonderful scenes of nature around Syracuse. They must have seen time after time that sapphire sea, the flower-enamelled fields of Achradina. And if the time came when after cruel torture and pain " weeping her shining eyes she turned away," it was surely not merely from the pangs of martyrdom that those lovely orbs were suffused with tears, but through grief at having to close for ever their sight upon an earth so fair, so enchanting, as Syracuse, the home of her birth and her death.

Christmas Festivities. The Festivity of the Nativity of Christ was appointed to be celebrated on December 25th, sometime during the fourth century of our era. The date coincided with the *dies natalis soli invicti,* the birthday of the unconquered sun in the Mithraic religion. Among the elements that symbolise Christmas in Italy are the *presepi* or holy manger scenes. These representations, which hold a place of their own in the history of art, are perhaps best seen at Naples, where they reached a wonderful peak of development in their various forms. (The

Museum of San Martino contains some outstanding exhibits of *presepios*, the most remarkable one being the " Sacred Crib," containing hundreds of figurines by Cuciniello, the greatest Neapolitan specialist in this branch of art.) Other impressive displays will be found at Amalfi, Caserta, Rome and Vico Equense.

Another Christmas symbol is the crib. Tradition says that St. Francis set up the first crib at Greccio in 1223. There is also the *ceppo*, or Christmas candle, which burns from Christmas Eve until the New Year. In the more remote parts of Italy, this tradition is maintained in various forms. In the Tuscan Apennines, for instance, the children circle about it blindfold, while they recite the *Ave Maria del ceppo*. Then, there is the poetry of the burning log which is very much felt in the Abruzzo. In Tuscany, too, the feast of the Christmas log is epitomised by the lighting of the classic stump of wood which, however, is in the form of a little hut.

Food figures largely in the Christmas celebrations, with local gastronomic dishes being served. The *capitone* is usually *de rigueur*. It is a tenacious eel, for even in the frying pan and broken up into fragments, it twists and vibrates, minus its head. Sometimes it arrives on the table emitting its death rattle. On the other hand, this unspeakable tenacity, as soon as it is defeated, is compensated for by a tender, white, and very sweet dish. Other local specialities include the *panettone* of Milan, the *torrone* of Cremona and Benevento, the *bicciolani* of Vercelli, and *biscotti* of Novara, and the *cassata* of Palermo, not to mention the *panforte*, the *ricciarelli* and the *cavallucci* of Siena, the *pizzicati* of Perugia, the *befanotti* of Lucca, the *pane di saba* of Sassari, the *pignolata* of Messina, the *struffoli* of Naples and Southern Latium, the *canditi* of Genoa and the *cicerchiata* of the Abruzzi region—but there are dozens more, all helping to make Christmas in Italy the sweetest time of the year, in every way.

Christmas in Milan opens with the famous **Fair of St. Ambrogio,** called *Oh Bei* ! *Oh Bei* ! which is held in the square of the same name and lasts 15 days. It is a picturesque conglomeration of stalls displaying the most diverse wares from ceramics to fabrics, toys to pictures darkened with age.

Special **Christmas Services** are held throughout Italy, among the outstanding ones being in Rome. Here is a list of some of the more unusual celebrations:

Armenian Rite, San Nicola da Tolentino.
Catholic/Greek rite, Sant' Atanasio.
Russo-Slav rite, San Lorenzo ai Monti.
Maronite rite, San Marone, Via Aurora.
Russian language, S. Antonio dell' Esquilino.
Rumanian language, San Salvatore alle Coppelle.
Armenian, Mechitarist Chapel at Sant' Anselmo.
Antiochan, Sant' Efrem.

Byzantine-Slav rite, Sant' Antonio Abate.

Old Slav, San Giosafat Ieromartire.

Greek-Byzantine rite, San Basilio.

Syro-Antiochan rite, Santa Maria in Campo Marzio.

Sumptuous vestments in brightly-coloured brocade, tall mitres resplendent with gold, long hooked pastoral staffs, golden crosses studded with jewels, and spectacular staging accompanied by solemn music composed many centuries ago by the most famous figures of the Eastern Church cannot fail to leave on the visitor impressions which must surely last a lifetime. And it is only in Rome with its universality that such a variety of religious ceremonies is possible.

A feature, too, of Rome at Christmastime is the bagpipe players, who are, traditionally, shepherds from the Abruzzi. Mention must also be made of the Basilica of Aracoeli where during the Christmas Mass the statue of the Holy Child is carried in procession to the accompaniment of dirges played on bagpipes. This church is also famous for its *presepios*, but these will be found in many other Roman churches.

Of unusual interest is the **Mass of the Sword** in the ancient Basilica of Aquileia (near Trieste). While he is reading the Gospel, the priest grasps a sword as a symbol of the civil and spiritual power of the venerable Patriarchate of Aquileia. This one-time famous port, now a mere hamlet, has some of the most interesting monuments, and although almost unknown to tourists it is not difficult to reach. Christmas Mass is celebrated according to the traditional Byzantine rite at Piana Degli Albanesi, when the women wear their splendidly rich costumes.

Finally, at Revine Lago (Vittorio Veneto) on December 25th and January 6th the whole population of the town, in costume, take part in the **Celebration of the Living Holy Manger.** The shepherds dressed in sheep skins pay homage to the Baby Jesus, coming down in procession from the mountains. On the plain, fires of twigs are lit to illuminate the road for the Magi; forecasts for the new year's harvests are made from the direction of the smoke. And I must mention a personal favourite Christmas Eve ceremony: at Taormina when shepherds come down the surrounding mountainside bearing young lambs. After Midnight Mass in the town everyone joins in an open-air picnic.

PILGRIMAGES

Rome is, of course, the outstanding goal of world pilgrimages; but there are no definite dates, except for the opening of the Holy Gate every 25 years—the last occasion was in 1950.

The following six pilgrimages can be said to rank amongst the most important, drawing crowds of pilgrims from every part of the world:

The **Sanctuary of the Holy House (Santa Casa) of Loreto (Ancona),** standing on a hill wherefrom a large sweep of the Adriatic coast and the towns of Recanati and Castelfidardo can be seen. It is held that the Holy House is no less than the house where the Madonna was born, carried by angels from Nazareth first to Raunizza (Yugoslavia) and then to a wood near Recanati. The Sanctuary contains precious works by Melozzo da Forlì, Luca Signorelli, Giuliano and Benedetto da Maiano. Anniversary: December 10th, date of the removal of the Holy House.

Santa Maria Degli Angeli, near Assisi. The history of this Sanctuary, located in an area of surpassing beauty, is linked with Saint Francis, who obtained it from the Benedictines with a portion of land (hence the name of Porziuncola). The magnificent temple, built in the second half of the 17th century as it now looks, is full of reminders of the " Poverello " of Assisi. Anniversary: August 1st and 2nd, solemnity of the Pardon.

The **Basilica of Sant' Antonio da Padova,** Padua. The extraordinary popularity among the believers of the Santo to whom the Church is dedicated and the architectural beauty of the Basilica account for the great number of pilgrims who flock to Padua on innumerable occasions, but mostly in June, when recurs the calendar holiday of the Santo (June 13th). The body of the Saint is kept in the sumptuous Cappella dell'Arca. The Basilica was built in 1231, shortly after St. Antonio's death.

The **Sanctuary of the Beata Vergine del Rosario,** Pompeii. One of the most venerated Marian Sanctuaries the world over. Built in 1876, the first coronation ceremonies of the Madonna of the Rosary took place in 1887. Popes, kings and princes donated the church sacred vestments, jewels and priceless gems. Anniversary: May 8th, date of the Coronation, and First Sunday of October, Feast of the Rosary.

The **Sanctuary of Monte Berico,** Vicenza, amid magnificent scenery. The temple was erected after two miraculous visions (1426 and 1428) of the Virgin at a time when plague raged the city of Vicenza. Besides the Oratory, the church dates from 1518. The view from the Sanctuary esplanade is superb. Anniversary: March 7th and August 25th, date of the Visions.

The **Sanctuary of the Madonna Della Salute,** Venice. The lofty, imposing cupola and the harmonious architecture, the work of Longhena, are an attraction in themselves. It dates from 1630. An image of the Madonna is venerated. Francesco Morosini saved it from profanation by the Moslems of Crete and brought it to Venice when the Sanctuary was being built. Anniversary: April 23rd, date of the Coronation.

SPORTING FIXTURES

Some of the most unusual sporting events in Italy, such as the Palio at Siena and the Football Game in Florence are more in the nature of traditional customs and are dealt with under that heading.

Among the modern events, the **Mille Miglia** (1,000 miles race) in May-June is traditionally the longest and the hardest race in Europe for sporting motor-cars, but is now a speed-and-efficiency race. Its route starts in Brescia and, running through Northern and Central Italy and across the Apennines it reaches Rome and Naples, and then returns to Brescia along the Adriatic coast. This race, rich in sporting thrills, passes through several ancient cities, and it receives participation by manufacturers of international repute.

Other important motor-car races and competitions are:

Grand Prix of Italy, followed by the **Motorcycling Grand Prix of the Nations,** Monza, September.

Targa Florio, Palermo, May 1st.

Spring Motor Rally, Merano, April.

Circuit of Garda, April.

Uphill Speed Race, Pontedecimo (Genoa)—Giovi, September.

Uphill Speed Race, Trento-Bondone, July.

Rally of the European Capitals, Rome, April.

Grand Prix, Syracuse, April 25th.

Important horse shows (including jumping) are those at Como (May), Rome (May), Turin (March), while among horse racing events the outstanding ones are the **Grand Prix,** Merano, September, which is linked with an important national lottery, and the **Trotting Grand Prix of Agnano,** Naples, June, also linked with a big lottery.

Yachting regattas are held at Genoa (March); the most important in the Mediterranean is at Naples (August); and the **Regatta Della Giraglia,** San Remo to Toulon, circles Corsica.

There are also: **International Sailing Week,** Riva del Garda, July; the **Palio of the Gulf,** a rowing contest at La Spezia, August; and **Sailors' Palio,** Leghorn, August.

Other sporting events worth noting are:

World Bob Sleigh Championships, Cortina d'Ampezzo, January.

International Tennis Tournament, Cava dei Tirreni, August.

International Tennis Tournament, San Benedetto del Tronto, August.

The classic **100 km. Walking Race,** Lecco (Como), November.

An annual event which thrills most Italians is the **Giro d'Italia,** a long-distance cycling race (May/June).

And I would also like to add the **International Dog Shows** at Nervi (April), at Bologna, Florence and Milan (May), Trieste (June), Bellagio (September), while there are **Trials for Hunting Dogs** at Bolgheri (Leghorn), Treviso, Como, Arezzo, and Cavaglioni (Siena).

TRADITIONAL CUSTOMS
January

One of the most deafening occasions in all Europe is the **Befana** (night of January 5th) held in the Piazza Navona, Rome. Wooden stalls are set up in the Square for the sale of toys and sweets. Gay crowds, including many children, gather and remain there until the early hours, with much noise from toy trumpets and whistles. Traditionally, *La Befana* is a kindly but sharp-eyed old hag, who visits the houses of children by night, leaving presents for the good children. This feast coincides with that of the Epiphany, an ancient ceremony linked with the Wise Men, and it has the same significance as we give to Christmas. It is, indeed, a day marking the start of the new year. Celebrations are also held on this night in Trastevere, Rome, as well as in many parts of Italy, with children dressed in costume and going from door to door singing carols and receiving, in exchange for their music, gifts of eggs, sweets and nuts.

At Tarcento (Udine) **Epiphany Celebrations** comprise a group of interesting festivities which, according to ancient tradition, culminate in a torchlight procession to the top of a hill where there is a bonfire. The progress of agriculture for the year is forecast from the coils of smoke exuding from the bonfire. Dances and the singing of traditional songs complete the ceremony.

February

Almond Blossom Festival,* Agrigento, February 5th to 14th. This is a superb spectacle held in a valley bounded by ancient Greek temples against the background of the eternally blue sea. There are many folklore performances, including a variety of songs in the Sicilian dialect and various regional dances. The biggest marvel, however, are the almond blossoms which enhance the Temples like scenery on a stage. The arrival of Spring in Agrigento (when other regions are still in the grip of winter) is an incomparable, unique vision.

Feast of the Matriculation, Padua, February. Every year the university students celebrate with noisy humour and solemnity this Feast, which is a continuation of a very ancient tradition. The occasion is celebrated in various university cities, but it has a particular liveliness in Padua, and there the whole of the population joins in, while delegations of students come from other parts of the country. The students pass through the streets in noisy groups wearing their characteristic hats of many colours. Their general headquarters is the famous Café Pedrocchi.

Sa Sartiglia, Oristano (Cagliari), February 28th to March 1st. This is a medieval-type joust in which, after various ceremonies, the masked knights on horseback, one after the other, attempt to plunge their lances into a star suspended in the air.

March

Segavecchia, Forlimpopoli (Forli), mid-Lent.   This ancient traditional festival presents a colossal female puppet adorned with necklaces of dried fruit seated on a dais in the public square or carried around on a cart and afterwards sawn.   During the procession young couples in love in front of the puppet receive a good omen for their wedding.

A similar event is the **Festival of the Old Lady** at Brescia and at Bergamo, terminating in a singular gastronomic contest with spaghetti and polenta.

In the regions of Southern Italy, dolls made of rags representing the old lady, said to be the wife of Carnival, are hung over the doors of houses.   Each doll has seven feathers indicating the seven weeks of Lent and one of them is detached every week.

Jousting the Bear, Pistoia, March 10th.   The joust strictly speaking is a combat between two knights charging each other with lances.   In Pistoia the game of *La Giostra dell' Orso* is held in the Cathedral Square. It is of very ancient origin, and in it 12 competing horsemen, representing four town districts, proceed to the jousting-place, accompanied by a brilliantly costumed retinue.   Then, two by two, with lowered lances, they race at headlong gallop towards the effigies of two bears and tilt at the targets displayed in the outstretched paws.   Points are conferred for every hit, and the winning team receives the coveted rewards, while the successful champion is proclaimed " Knight of the Golden Spur of Pistoia."

April

Serenade of " Calendimaggio," Assisi, April 29th to 30th.   This is an outstanding event, and it is linked with the memory of St. Francis. The city is divided for the occasion into two sections, each being represented by long processions of *messeri* (gentlemen) and *madonne* (ladies) who are escorted by Knights and Esquires; they gaily compete with each other in the Piazza del Comune in singing and music to give a worthy welcome to the entry of May, the month of Love.   According to early biographers, St. Francis used to sing serenades through the city streets at night.   During one of these he had the vision of the " Madonna Poverta."

Procession of the " Real Maestranza," Caltanissetta, Holy Thursday. This is a procession of the craftsmen's guilds, the members of which are dressed in black and carry lighted candles.   This festivity is linked with religious ceremonies, referred to elsewhere.

" Scoppio del Carro " (Explosion of the Cart), Florence, Easter Saturday.   During the singing of the Gloria a cart containing explosives is first drawn in procession through the streets by white oxen, and is then ignited by the sacred fire borne to it by a mechanical dove liberated at the high altar of the Cathedral, and with its explosion Easter begins. The explosion augurs well for the future harvest. The event recalls the victorious return from the first Crusade.

Festival of the " Spadonari " (swordsmen), various places, St. George's Day. Various towns and villages claim St. George as their patron saint, and celebrate accordingly. In some places in the Susa Valley, the Festival of the Swordsmen takes place. It is a re-evocation of a people's revolt against a feudatory who extorted money from those under his dominion. It culminates in a dance by young men of the town who wear characteristic costumes and carry menacing sabres.

Race of the Oxen, Caresana (Vercelli), St. George's Day. In honour of St. George who liberated the town from a terrible plague in the 17th century, four ox-carts, driven by fearless young men, are sent along a track in a race. A similar race of oxen is held at Asigliano (Vercelli) during the first ten days of May.

Festival of the Rosebud, Venice, April 25th. A charming tradition dictates that on the day of St. Mark the young men of Venice must present a rosebud to the girls they love. Therefore St. Mark's day is also called the " festival of the rosebud."

May

Sagra del Pesce (Fish Festival), Camogli (Genoa), second Sunday in May. On St. Fortunato's Day, this picturesque seaport holds a recently instituted festival when portions of fish are cooked in a colossal frying-pan on the water-front, with pretty girls dishing it out free to all those present, while a band plays and there is general gaiety. An attempt to duplicate this feast at Passignano sul Trasimeno (Perugia) has terminated, because of the transport difficulty in bringing the loaned pan from Camogli.

Sardinian Cavalcade,* Sassari, Ascension Day. One of the outstanding events in Europe, and also one of the most complete surveys of Italian folklore. Its origins date back to the final years of Spanish rule in Sardinia, that is in 1711. The whole of Sardinia participates, and over 60 towns and villages take part in their traditional costumes. There is a wonderful display of chromatic ranges of colours in the dresses, some of which indicate the survival of very ancient Egyptian and Byzantine influences. A similar procession of Sardinian costumes is to be seen in Nuoro on the occasion of the **Feast of the Redeemer** (August), while on Sundays and feast-days wonderful displays of traditional dress can be seen in Desulo, Oliena, Orgosolo and Dorgali (province of Nuoro) and Osilo and Ittiri (province of Sassari).

Il Gioco del Calcio, (Football Match), Florence, first Sunday in May and June 24th. This exciting and historic football match takes place in the Piazza della Signoria, and the players wear 16th-century costumes.

It is an historical evocation of the match played on February 17th, 1530, as a mark of defiance against the troops of Charles V who were besieging the city. Each team consists of 27 players, and the match is preceded by an Historical Procession in costume. The winning team is awarded the traditional prize of a fat calf.

Festival of the Cricket, Florence, Ascension Day. This characteristic Florentine festival is held in the immense Cascine Public Gardens. Salesmen offer the *grilli* in small cages, but the origin of this event came from the time when teams of " beaters " were organised to destroy the swarms of crickets that were damaging the crops in this area. During this " Operation Cricket " there was great merriment and special picnic feasting. Even when the crickets were destroyed, this festival was still maintained.

Race of the Ceri (Candles), Gubbio, mid-May. A unique festival probably originating in pre-Christian days; its date corresponds to the Ides of May in the pagan calendar. The " candles," which originally were made of wax, were later exchanged for the weighty and tower-like structures of wood reinforced by iron bands (weighing 4½ cwt. each) that we see now. They are taken in procession to the Piazza dei Consoli, where the teams of bearers pause to rest. Then, at a signal are transported at a run to the top of Monte Igino, where they are offered to St. Ubaldo. It is an exciting race, while Gubbio itself is one of the most enchanting of Umbrian towns. In its Town Hall there are the famous Eugubian Tables, dating from 200 B.C. and providing a key to the primitive Umbrian language. The town is also famed for its majolica ware.

Concluding the week of festivities in which the *Ceri* takes place, there is also the **Palio dei Balestrieri** (Crossbowmen). This traditional Contest in Costume has its origins in a medieval dispute between the Crossbowmen of Gubbio and those of Sansepolcro. To-day the contest is keenly fought between teams of archers, including some from abroad. There is a colourful display of medieval pomp, with a costumed procession. The winner is invested with the title of " Chief Bowman " and is entitled to hold for a year the coveted *Pallium*, or mantle of honour, which he must for a certain number of days display at one of the windows or the door of his house in token of his victory.

June

Procession of the Decorated Horse, Brindisi, Corpus Christi. This traditional event dates back to the period of the Crusades when, legend claims, the vessel of the French king, bearing with him the Eucharist, was wrecked on the beach at Brindisi. The archbishop at that time went to fetch the sacred relic which he carried in procession, mounted on a richly caparisoned white horse. To commemorate this event the Archbishop of Brindisi proceeds in procession carrying the

Most Holy Relic; he rides a horse covered with gold drapery and having a golden saddle, and passes under galleries of silk draperies and a rain of flowers.

Feast of the " Gigli " (Lilies), Nola, mid-June. The name derives from the fact that originally real lilies were used, attached to reeds woven together; they were later replaced by the present eight very high wooden objects (98 ft. high and weighing about 50 cwt. each) which are covered with paintings and statues of saints, but the decorative motifs vary from year to year. These machines, each requiring 40 bearers, are carried in procession through the streets, in a dance rhythm. The festival commemorates a welcome given to a bishop by the people on his return from prison.

Palio of the Goose and River Festival,* Pavia, end of June. This takes place in one of the most appealing art cities of Italy, and it is within easy reach of Milan. This tournament of skill is devoted to the " Leap of the Goose," originating from the Middle Ages as a test of swimming skill for local boatmen. On the evening of June 28th, a man clad as the Duke Gian Galeazzo Maria Visconti, the Lord of 14th century Pavia and founder of the famous Carthusian Church (Certosa di Pavia), opens the gate of the Castle to the people. Each of the nine wards provides a wooden tower, and a " battle " follows between them.

The " Tournament of the Towers " takes place the same evening, each of the mobile towers being manned by a garrison of six men. Five act as bearers of their tower, while the sixth man stands at the top as the warrior. With his lance he tries to hit a circle painted on one side of an opposing tower. The worst hit tower collapses. The fight continues until eight towers have collapsed, the remaining intact tower being the winner. But they have still to compete in a final battle: the conquest of the Beccaria Tower, access to which is limited to three gang-planks and defended by men of the " Rione del Centro." If the assailants win, the tower is set alight. In the afternoon of June 29th, there is a spectacular historical procession through the streets towards the river, and with some live geese carried in cages. (The geese form part of another historical legend dating back to the time when the Gauls besieged the city, and these birds acted as efficient sentries.)

Once at the river's bank, the competition for the Palio starts. It is a combined row-and-swim relay race, both up and downstream. At the end of the itinerary there is a raft from which the competitors take a jump at a goose suspended in the air. If missed, no further attempt can be made. In the evening, there is a blaze of fireworks. Altogether, this is one of the most unusual and interesting of Italian festivals.

Fight for the Bridge,* **Illuminations of San Ranieri,*** **Regatta of San Ranieri,** Pisa, all held in June. The *Giuoco del Ponte* (June 4th) is an evocation of the Game which took place in the 13th century. Two competing teams, in costume, with about 800 persons take part. Following a procession, 24 men of each army line up along a mechanism on rails and push. The side that makes the goal on the enemy side wins, and this is repeated five times.

Some days later (June 16th) a ceremony takes place at the City Hall when the winners are presented with the prize, a *palio*, silken banner. That night a big celebration (the **Holiday of St. Ranieri**) takes place, with illuminations in every house. Pisa is ablaze, with thousands of small wax lights (called *lampadini*) arranged in small wooden bowls on the sides of houses. The effect is magical, especially where the lights are reflected on the waters of the River Arno. This, in fact, is the most famous celebration of its kind in the whole world.

The historical Regatta of San Ranieri (June 17th) takes place in costume between representatives of the four city quarters.

La Giostra del Saracino, * Arezzo, first Sunday in June, also in September. This is the most famous of Italian jousts. It originated during the Crusades, when it was used as a form of propaganda to popularise the fight against the infidel and the reconquest of Jerusalem. Eight Knights, respresenting the four city quarters, accompanied by a picturesque retinue of horsemen, drummers, mace-bearers, footmen, and cross-bowmen, march to the lists, where there has been set up the effigy of a Moor, armed with a shield and a heavy flail held in the right hand. The Knights must try to hit the Saracen's shield in the centre with their lances without being touched by the cruel weapon. The winner receives the golden lance on behalf of his district.

Festival of the Strawberries, Nemi, second Sunday in June. This pleasant village, 20 miles from Rome and situated beside the lake of the same name, is a perfect setting for this characteristic Spring festival. The Festival of the Strawberries is full of rustic charm and savour, and attracts big crowds. The programme is very interesting: in the morning there is a parade of beautiful girls in the typical costumes of the place, who carry baskets full of strawberries; in the afternoon baskets and strawberries are given away to all visitors, and this is followed by a procession of allegorical floats, mandoline contests, dances, singing, and, to close the festivities, contests of fireworks.

July

Palio of the Contrade, * Siena, July 2nd and August 16th. One of the world's most interesting and most important folklore festivals, it has been held without interruption since the 15th century in its present form and ritual. *Palio* comes from the Latin *pallium*, a cloak, which was the award in contests, usually equestrian, in olden days. All through the Middle Ages these contests, in various forms, were highly popular. The main event is a race of ten horses (representing ten out of the 17 districts into which the city is divided) three times round the principal, shell-shaped square of the city. The event is preceded by a parade and flag-waving display in costume, as well as the evocative ceremony of blessing the horses in the Cathedral. The horsemen race bareback and are allowed to strike at one another with their whips. The prize is a piece of coloured silk on which are worked the figure of the Virgin and the city emblems. The festivities at night in the winning district are also very unusual. Altogether, I would claim that this is the most fascinating historical spectacle in Italy, possibly in the world.

Feast of Santu Antine, Sedilo (Cagliari), July 5th to 7th. The focal point of this festival is the Joust of the Ardia that takes place at 6 p.m. on the 6th and is repeated at 7 a.m. on the 7th, in honour of the Saint who won the battle of Saxa Rubra against Maxentius.

August

Joust of the Quintana, Ascoli Piceno, early August. In this outstanding minor art city there is an historical performance with 700 persons in 15th century costume. There are offerings of candles, benediction of the horses and of the Palio, a flag-waving contest, race of the ring, and the tournament of the Quintana. In the evening there is a fascinating torchlight procession.

International Folklore Festival, Pescara, mid-August. One of the events constituting a Motor Week which is held every year in this delightful Adriatic town, and it has become the most important contest of its kind in Italy.

Landing of the Saracens, Positano, August 11th. A romantic revival of the times when the Saracens used to invade this coast. The mock landing is accompanied by fireworks, etc., which enhance the beauty and the fascination of the scene in this attractive seaside resort.

The " Giants," Messina, August 13th and 14th. " Mata " and " Grifone " are two giants on a horseback, made of *papier mâché* and wood, and are 30 ft. high. They symbolise the mythical founders of Messina, and as they are drawn through the streets, " Mata " on a black horse, " Grifone " riding a white horse, they are enthusiastically greeted.

The " Vara," Messina, August 15th. This procession has as its main feature the *Vara*, an imposing machine in the form of a pyramid which raises on its summit the Virgin. It is drawn by hundreds of the faithful, and as it moves along, the tableau comes to life by means of internal mechanism. The clouds move in every direction, the golden sun and silver moon, and the angels make a deep impression on the spectators. Until 1860, all the figures were alive and in past centuries the young girl who impersonated the Virgin could request mercy for someone condemned to death. Today, only the figures manipulating the lower platform are human beings.

Graziella, Procida, August. This is a true " Festival of the Sea."
The islanders engage in a marine palio and a contest for fishing boats,
while the procession of the Assumption descends from Mount Procida
to the open sea where the Madonna meets St. Michael. Folklore dances
in typical costumes follow. There is also a picturesque procession of
lampare (boats), and, finally, there is the election of the *Graziella*, the most
beautiful girl on the island, who receives the name of Lamartine's tearful
heroine.

September

Joust of the Saracen, Arezzo, September (see description in June).

Chess Game in Costume, Marostica (Vicenza), mid-September.
This recalls a legend to the effect that two rivals competed with each
other in a chess match for the hand of a girl. Living persons are used
as pawns.

Festival of Piedigrotta,* Naples, September 7th to 9th. This is an
explosion of fiery and musical joy, spurred by plenty of wine. There
is nothing in Italy to beat this violently gay affair. For three days and
nights Naples is ablaze with lights and bright with decorations. There
are two legends that relate to its origin: one narrates that it commemorates the destruction in A.D. 44 of a site that had hitherto been the
scene of pagan orgies, and the erection thereon of a chapel; while the
second version states that the chapel was built in 1356 after the Blessed
Virgin Mary had appeared to a priest, a nun and a certain Peter and
ordered its construction. The noise and gaiety of this *festa* pervade the
whole town, and should you be allergic to noise, then I advise you to
stay away, for you will certainly get little sleep. Apart from the processions and fireworks, this is also an opportunity to see some fascinating
puppet shows.

Jousting the Bear, Pistoia, early September (for description
see March).

La Giostra della Quintana, Foligno, September. First held in
1613, the Joust of the Quintain lapsed, but was revived in 1646, since
when it has become an annual event. It takes place in the main square,
where ten competing horsemen, garbed in 17th century costumes, cover
at a gallop a course laid out in the shape of a figure of eight, and then,
with their lances, strike at the head of the Quintain, or a wooden effigy
of a knight. The district whose champion secures the highest score is
presented with a richly decorated *pallium*, which it holds until the following year.

Historical Regatta,* Venice, first Sunday of September. For
splendour th s celebration ranks with the Siena Palio. The Regatta has
seven centuries of history; and it is a competition in speed for small
gondolas with two oars and a crew in costume. The Grand Canal used

for the course is decked with flags, banners, tapestries, etc. It is preceded by a procession of historical boats, all richly decorated and strewn with flowers. Leading this cavalcade is the historic *bucintoro* (a great parade vessel with oars and luxurious carvings and golden sculptures) carrying the authorities and the representatives of the four Maritime Republics in costume with standards. The races arouse intense enthusiasm, and on their completion all the canals become crowded with boatloads of folk making gay in noisy disorder. This, in fact, is the loveliest rowing competition in the world.

Millenary Fair, Gonzaga (Mantua), early September. It is believed that this Fair was instituted in 1498 and it is a characteristic institution. Nowadays it is mainly agricultural, but its opening brings a procession of ladies and knights in costume with a picturesque display of heralds and standard-bearers.

October

Truffle Fair, Alba, during month. This autumn gastronomic event to spread the popularity of the truffle, which is one of the typical products of the district, is really a fair of sorts, but it is the only one of its kind in Italy. It is very colourful, for it is the occasion for folk dances, bands, and a truffle contest, all combined with gargantuan consumption of food and local wines. Not recommended, however, for anyone on a diet !

Fair of San Luca, L'Impruneta (near Florence), middle of October during the Festival of St. Luca. There is the bustle and merriment of a three-day fair which reaches its peak on the second day, the Tuesday, with what is called the " Fierone," when succulent, Pantagruel-like portions of roast chicken are eaten on the Mount of the Sante Marie.

December

Exhibition of the Red Radish of Treviso, Treviso. This is held every year under the historic loggia of the 14th century Palace.

TRADE FAIRS

Outstanding trade fairs in Italy include:

International Samples Fair, Milan, last fortnight in April.

Mediterranean Fair, Palermo, May 25th to June 10th.

Levant Fair, Bari, September.

Fashion Collections, Florence, January and July.

International Citrus Fair, Reggio Calabria, late March to early April.

National Handicrafts Exhibition, Florence, June.

International Foodstuffs Salon, Bologna, May.

International Milk Fair and National Agricultural Fair, Cremona, September.

International Motor-car Show, Turin, November.

International Salon of Technology, Turin, September-October.
International Exhibition of Electronics, Atomic Energy, Radio and Cinema, Rome, June.
Triennale Display of Decorative Arts, Milan, held every third year. Of outstanding importance.

For full information apply to the Italian Chamber of Commerce, 31, Old Burlington Street, London, W.1.

WINE FESTIVALS

The harvesting of the grape is celebrated everywhere in Italy where there are vineyards. During September and October mention can be made of such festivals at Acireale, Capri, Frascati, Ravello, Soave and Sorrento. Two outstanding events take place at Chianti (Tuscany) and at Marino (Castelli Romani, near Rome). At the last named, free wine gushes from a fountain.

CHAPTER SEVENTEEN

Liechtenstein

THIS LILLIPUTIAN PRINCIPALITY, THE LAST REMAINING LAND TO be under Hapsburg rule, is wedged between Switzerland's eastern border and the Austrian province of Vorarlberg. It holds its National Day on August 15th, the birthday of the Ruling Prince. The firework display on this occasion is said to be the finest in Central Europe. At 9 p.m. the Prince and his family come down from their home, a medieval castle which dominates the town, to mingle with his people. Another interesting celebration is the " Cow Festival " held in mid-September. This is the occasion of the cows returning from their alpine summer pastures, and the heroine of the procession is the cow that has given the most milk. Readers of Paul Gallico's book " Ludmila " will find a full account of this charming event.

CHAPTER EIGHTEEN

Luxembourg

THIS ENCHANTING LITTLE DUCHY IS ONE OF THE MOST RESTFUL places I know in Europe. It has a gentle beauty and a warm-hearted people, and here you will always find time to stop and stare in surroundings which make it a worthwhile pastime.

Of Luxembourg's annual events, undoubtedly the most outstanding is the strange religious Dancing Procession at Echternach on Whit Tuesday—an excellent centre for walking excursions in unspoilt countryside.

Great Procession of Pilgrimage to Our Lady of Luxembourg, Luxembourg City, fifth Sunday after Easter. Thousands of people travel to the shrine of Our Lady in the cathedral of Luxembourg City to ask her blessing, from the third to fifth Sundays after Easter. A great closing procession ends this pilgrimage as thousands of people walk through the flower-festooned city, most of them dressed in black in sharp contrast to the bright banners draping the streets and the colourful robes of the dignitaries. The Grand Ducal Family, members of Government, Diplomatic Corps and other authorities all take part in this big closing ceremony.

Floral Paradise, Mondorf-Les-Bains, end of April to early May. Flower show.

Broom and Gorse Festival, Wiltz, Whit Monday. A colourful gorse parade makes its way through streets that glow with yellow blooms. After the election of the Gorse Queen, dancing and amusements take place in the evening.

Dancing Procession, Echternach, Tuesday after Whit Monday. This unusual religious ceremony is without doubt the best known event beyond the borders of Luxembourg. It honours St. Willibrord, surprisingly enough a British missionary from Northumberland, though the celebration was probably in existence already in pagan times. The procession starts in the morning, to the pealing of bells. Leading it are priests, choristers, men carrying crosses and banners, and choir-boys; then comes an orchestra of young boys, mostly playing violins, guitars and mandolines. They are followed by the dancers in white shirts and short trousers holding each other by the hand or by a handkerchief knotted at both ends. And while the traditional chant rings out, they come leaping forward. Finally, there follows the long procession of pilgrims. But these people do not walk or march—they dance, five steps forward and three backward, all the way, to the strange melody played by the musicians. It is one of the most unusual religious ceremonies in Europe and, once seen, not easy to forget.

International Trade and Industries Fair, Luxembourg City, end of May to early June.

Wine Fairs. Several take place during the spring and summer, usually consisting of wine tastings followed by dancing and amusements. Such a Fair is held at Wellenstein on the second Thursday before Easter. Others are: at Grevenmacher, the Thursday after Easter; at Remerschen, May 1st; at Wormeldange, the Thursday after Whitsun, and at Remich on July 21st.

International Theatre Festival, Wiltz, end of July to early August. Open air performances of operettas and dramas in French and German, with well-known foreign artists, are staged against the lovely background of the old castle.

Great Annual Amusement Fair, Luxembourg City, end of August to early September. Traffic stops completely in the centre of the city as every business house, from the smallest shop to the largest store, empties its wares on to open air stalls along the streets.

Wine Feasts. Held in the wine-growing towns of the Moselle district during September or early October. At Schwebsingen, on the first Sunday in September, wine flows from a wine fountain.

CHAPTER NINETEEN

Malta

THE MOST COLOURFUL AND INTERESTING EVENTS IN MALTA usually occur in conjunction with religious feast days in honour of a national or local saint, of which the island has many.

CARNIVALS

Shrovetide Carnivals, all over Malta, three days before Lent. Three days of merrymaking, characterised by parades, fancy dress balls and feasts. Biggest and best of the processions is the one in Valetta, where you will find the whole gamut of grotesque masks, comic groups, decorated floats and marching bands. Dancing on the Palace Square includes the Maltese national dance, the *contradanza,* but Carnival Balls, known as *veljuni,* are held everywhere, lasting well into the early hours of the morning.

NATIONAL OR SPECIAL DAYS

National Day, all over Malta, September 8th. This falls on the feast day of Our Lady of Victories, and celebrations last for three days. The Archbishop holds a Requiem Mass at St. John's Cathedral, bands play in the main squares and Valetta is illuminated and decorated. The colourful *dghajsas,* the gondola-like boats of Malta, feature prominently in a regatta held in the Grand Harbour, Valetta.

RELIGIOUS EVENTS

Good Friday Processions, all over Malta. Far into the night, long processions through villages all over the island bear statues commemorating Our Lord's Death and Passion, to the accompaniment of funeral marches. The most impressive is held at Qormi.

Festas. Every village has its parish saint—sometimes more than one—and every saint is honoured by his or her own *festa* or feast day. A full programme of illuminations, street decorations, band music and fireworks has its climax in a religious procession bearing a statue of the parish saint. Firework displays in Malta are usually outstanding, no doubt an echo from the days when fireworks were made at home and the louder and longer the battery lasted, the greater it was considered the praise to the saint being honoured! *Festas* held near the sea usually include the traditional greasy pole at the top of which local stalwarts attempt to fix a flag.

One or more *festas* is celebrated in one centre or another almost every Sunday of the year, but the more important are as follows:

St. Paul's Shipwreck at Valetta, Valetta, February 10th.

Feast of St. Publius, Floriana, 15 days after Easter. St. Publius was the first Bishop of Malta, consecrated by St. Paul.

Feast of St. Peter and St. Paul, Mdina, June 29th.

Our Lady of Victories, Senglea, Mellieha and Naxxar, September 8th, also the National Day, commemorating the lifting of two great sieges in 1565 and 1939-45.

TRADE FAIRS
Malta Trade Fair, Palazzo Parisio, Naxxar, July.

TRADITIONAL
Imnarja, Boschetto Gardens, near Mdina, June 28th. Wining, dining, singing, dancing and general merrymaking last through the soft Mediterranean night against the lovely garden setting. Festivities continue all the following day, thus coinciding with the Feast of St. Peter and St. Paul.

Traditional Horse and Donkey Races, Rabat, June 29th.

CHAPTER TWENTY

Norway

EVERYONE HAS HEARD OF THE AUSTERE BEAUTY OF NORWAY'S fjords flanked by rugged mountains, and of the charm of her long summer days. Surprisingly less known is the loveliness of her blossom time in May to early June when fruit trees in their thousands colour the fjord lands with a riot of bloom. Happily this period coincides with Norway's greatest cultural event, the Bergen International Festival, a tribute in music, folklore and drama to Edvard Grieg.

As the home of ski-ing—a Norwegian rock carving depicting a man on skis dates back 4,000 years—there are also several interesting winter sports events on Norway's annual calendar of events. The most important occur during the famous Holmenkoll Week in March.

CULTURAL EVENTS

Bergen International Festival, Bergen, end of May and early June. One of the four great Scandinavian music festivals, this fortnight in Bergen in honour of Edvard Grieg includes orchestral concerts, drama, folklore, ballet and exhibitions. The composer's grand piano comes into daily use once more during recitals held at his Troldhaugen home, near Bergen, now a museum. The Festival could hardly have a better setting, for this old Hanseatic town, once the capital of the country, has glorious surroundings.

Nobel Peace Prize Presentation, Oslo, December 10th.

NATIONAL OR SPECIAL DAYS

Independence Day, all over the country, May 17th. Every town and village has its procession, but main festivities are in Oslo where the Royal Family greets a big parade from the balcony of the Palace.

Midsummer Night's Eve, all over the country, June 23rd. Norwegians greet the longest day of the year with bonfires, fireworks and dancing. At folk museums in Oslo and Lillehammer, there are special folk dancing performances.

Fjord Blossom Time in Western Norway, May-early June. Thousands of fruit trees are in blossom.

RELIGIOUS EVENTS

Religious Easter Festival Week, Oslo, ending with Easter Monday. Special church concerts, religious plays, and tours of churches and museums.

SPORTING FIXTURES

Monolith Ski Race, Oslo, early January. Thousands of people watch this " cross-country " ski race right in the heart of the city. This opening event of the winter sports season takes place in Oslo's Frogner Park, peopled by the strange and controversial statues of Gustav Vigeland.

World's Greatest Herring Fisheries, off Alesund on the west coast, January to March. A spectators' sport for angling enthusiasts and others, when special boats take visitors out to mingle with the fishing fleet and watch the herring catches being hauled in.

Lofoten Cod Fisheries, Lofoten Isles, February-April. The world's richest cod fisheries attract over 25,000 fishermen in 5,000 fishing craft each year. Special tours in March by Bergen Line and Fred Olsen Line will take you to this floating hive of activity, where you will also have a chance to fish for cod. But take warm clothing and a stable stomach along with you !

Holmenkoll Week, Oslo, March. Norway's great international ski-ing week includes cross-country racing, downhill and slalom, and rises to a climax on the final day, **Holmenkoll Day,** with ski jumping contests attended by the Norwegian Royal Family and more than 100,000 spectators. The presentation of prizes at Oslo's City Hall is accompanied by a torchlight procession through the streets. Ski-ing enthusiasts should note, however, that the downhill and slalom events usually take place at another Norwegian centre, which can vary each year.

Birkebeiner Langrenn, Lillehammer to Rena, end of March. Anyone can take part in this 35-mile cross-country ski race—providing they can remain so long on skis ! This race has its roots in history, and retraces the steps of two Royalists, known as " Birch Legs " or Birkebeiner, when they carried the King's two-year-old son to safety from enemy hands 750 years ago.

Snow and Water Ski Competitions, Geiranger, July. An unusual combination of summer and winter sports on Geiranger fjord and the glaciers above it. Similar summer ski meets also are held at Trollstig (near Åndalsnes) and at Stryn.

International Fishing Festival, Stavanger, mid-August. A four-day event with many prizes awarded according to weight and size of catch. These included recently a special plaque given by a local newspaper for the ugliest fish ! The occasion is accompanied by a programme of folk dancing performances.

Hanko International Sailing Regatta is held every summer at the end of June, with helmsmen from all over the world competing. Among the competitors are the Royal family of Norway.

International Viking Rally, during second half of September. Participants start simultaneously from various towns and finish at Oslo, after 1,700 miles.

TRADE FAIRS

Scandinavian Design Cavalcade, Oslo, end of August to mid-September. Norwegian arts, crafts and industrial design on show in exhibitions and window displays.

TRADITIONAL CUSTOMS

Bossekop Spring Fair, Alta, mid-March. Hundreds of Norwegian Lapps in colourful costume from remote settlements gather to trade reindeer meat and furs for supplies with traders from Hammerfest. A similar event also takes place in December.

Lapp Weddings, Karasjok and Kautokeino, Easter. These two largest Lapp villages in Norwegian Lapland provide the snowy background for colourful wedding ceremonies each Easter.

Fana Folklore, Fana, near Bergen, three times a week from the end of May to early September. An evening excursion from Bergen brings you to this country festival for folk dancing performances and a meal served in traditional style.

Oslo Day, Oslo, June. The Norwegian capital, in carnival mood, becomes the scene of a colourful procession. " Miss Oslo " is elected and attends a giant open-air ball in front of the City Hall.

Oslok Eve, Stiklestad, July 29th. Although celebrated with bonfires in many parts of the country, the main event takes place at Stiklestad, north of Trondheim, where an historical play commemorates the death of Norway's martyr king, St. Olav, who fell in a battle there on July 29th, 1030.

Student Festivals are held in Oslo, Bergen and Trondheim following matriculation (September). There are joyous scenes.

Skibotn Fair, Skibotn, November. A fair and grand get-together for the Lapps of Norway, Sweden and Finland is also an occasion for religious meetings of the Laestadius Sect of the Lutheran Church. The Sect, founded by the Swede Laestadius in the last century, is remarkable for the way in which lay preachers stir their congregations into a strange state of frenzy.

CHAPTER TWENTY-ONE

Portugal

WITH VERY FEW EXCEPTIONS, ANNUAL EVENTS IN THIS LAND OF sunshine, sandy beaches and rugged mountain interior include the religious element to a varying, but usually marked degree. As it is virtually impossible to separate this element from festivities which might otherwise be termed as traditional or carnival, I have listed them all together, as far as possible in chronological order.

Certain features are common to most festivals, depending on the part of the country in which they occur. For example, the majority in southern Portugal include a cattle fair and/or bullfighting which, in Portugal, does not mean death to the bull. Folkloric groups are amongst the main attractions of festivals in the north of the country, frequently accompanied by a colourful market featuring local pottery, brass and copperware. Festivities in honour of local saints run into hundreds, and only the more important are included in this chapter.

Easter Celebration at the Shrine of Our Lady of Atalaia, Alcochete, Easter Sunday. A ceremony backed by 400 years of tradition.

Traditional Observance of Our Lord Jesus of The Wounds, Sesimbra, week-end early in May. For 400 years, the fishermen of this picturesque village resort have honoured their patron with one of the most beautiful processions in the country.

Great Pilgrimages to the Shrine of Our Lady of Fatima,* Fatima. Pilgrimages to this famous centre continue from May to October, but the two greatest take place on May 12th and 13th and October 12th and 13th. It was on May 13th, 1917, that three children first had a vision of Our Lady of the Rosary, who subsequently appeared on the 13th of every month until October. Pilgrims converge here in their hundreds of thousands every year from every corner of the world.

Traditional Academic Celebrations, Coimbra, towards end of May. Coimbra University celebrates graduation and the end of the school year with a colourful ceremony known as the " Burning of the Ribbons," the ribbons being those worn by students on their long, black capes, and varying in colour according to the nature of their studies. Nocturnal serenades, tournaments, dancing and parades are also included in the celebrations.

Festival of the Popular Saints, various parts of Lisbon on June

13th, 24th and 29th. Lisbon, for me, will always be remembered as a city of light; on several days during the second half of June, it becomes, too, a city of laughter as parades, dancing in the decorated streets, flower contests and fireworks all contribute towards popular festivities in honour of St. Anthony, St. John and St. Peter.

Portugal Day, a national holiday, June 10th.

Great Festival of the Red Waistcoat,* Vila Franca de Xira, week-end in July. A famous occasion in a famous province of stockbreeders. *Campinos*, or cowboys, parade in colourful costume. Bulls are let loose in the streets, and catching them turns into a free-for-all ! Bullfights, folk dancing and singing, and a vast regional banquet all contribute to make this Vila Franca de Xira's big weekend of the year.

Great Festival and Fair of St. Walter (São Gualter), Guimarães, early August. Four days of processions, fireworks, bullfights and a big livestock fair. Main attraction is the Marcha Gualteriana, a costumed parade featuring folklore groups.

Festival of the Green Cap, Alcochete, Sunday in mid-August. Bullfights and other popular amusements.

Annual Fair and Pilgrimage of Our Lady of Agony, Viana do Castelo, lasting for eight days in August. One of the most outstanding religious and popular events in the north of Portugal, this attracts visitors from all over the country and neighbouring Spain. The costumed procession is superb and other events include bullfighting, parades, fireworks and dancing. Note that places from which to watch the procession are booked far in advance.

Pilgrimage of Our Lady of the Needy, Lamego, September 6th to 8th. This religious event is also celebrated as the town's Festival, a most colourful occasion.

Festival of Our Lord Jesus of the Needy and Annual Fair of St. Zita, Tomar, September 9th to 13th. An ancient and traditional event in one of the loveliest old cities of Portugal.

Festival of Our Lady of Good Voyage, Moita, mid-September. Religious ceremonies include a benediction of the fishing boats on the Sunday. Other events include bullfights and a fair.

Annual Fair of Our Lady of The Cape, Sesimbra, during third week in September. Organised by the local fishermen, the event is held at Cape Espichel, about eight miles from the little town. It dates back to the 13th century.

Annual Fair, Vila Franca de Xira, during first week in October. Including bullfights, a parade of *campinos* (cowboys) on horseback, and bull-fighting in the streets.

Annual Fair of Our Lady of Piety, Santarém, a fortnight in October. Perhaps the biggest fair in the stockbreeding province of

Ribatejo. Events include bullfights, cattle shows and many popular amusements.

Great Annual Fair of Grace, Sintra, October 18th and 19th.

Fair of St. Martin, Golegã, November 10th to 12th. Main feature is the famous Horse Show, which attracts horsemen and high society alike. This is certainly the place to see, *en masse*, the finest horses in the country.

CHAPTER TWENTY-TWO

Madeira

POPULAR SAINTS FESTIVAL, FUNCHAL, TEN DAYS IN JUNE. PROCESSIONS, fireworks, barbecues, and music competitions in the streets make this Madeira's leading summer event.

Festival of Our Lady of Monte, Monte, August 15th.

Great Festival of St. Sylvester,* all over the island, but particularly Funchal, December 31st. Fireworks and festivities echo far out over the Bay of Funchal, where ocean liners make a special call to enable passengers to witness the celebrations. The firework display must rank amongst the most impressive in the world.

CHAPTER TWENTY-THREE

San Marino

THIS TINY REPUBLIC WHICH LIES CLOSE TO RIMINI REPAYS A
short visit, for it claims to be the oldest as well as the smallest republic
in the world. It offers, too, some interesting festivals, including the **Feast
of San Marino** on September 5th. This is the celebration of the Republic;
there is a parade in costume, and the **Palio of the Crossbowmen** also
takes place on the same day. Then, twice a year, on March 15th and
September 15th, there are the curious elections of the two Captain-
Regents, which offer a fine picture of medieval pageantry. The age-long
ceremonies show off the particularly glorious and gorgeous costumes.

CHAPTER TWENTY-FOUR

Spain

SPAIN, BEING A COUNTRY OF MANY AND VARIED ASPECTS, STILL keeps most of its old traditions and local customs alive. Their diversity is due to the many different races that have invaded her: Phoenicians, Greeks, Barbarians, Romans, Arabs; and to differences of landscape and climate. But, please do not think of Spain purely in terms of bull-fights, flamenco dancing and mysterious hooded religious processions. All three certainly exist, but there are many other kinds of traditional festivals which illustrate other sides of life. They offer a richness which is as outstanding as in any other European land. Remember, though, that hotel accommodation for many festivals must be booked well in advance, while, quite legally, prices are raised, sometimes considerably, as at Holy Week and the Fair at Seville.

A Calendar of Events for each year is obtainable from the Spanish Tourist Office in London.

AGRICULTURAL AND LIVESTOCK FAIRS

While there is no central Agricultural Show in Spain, there are several interesting livestock markets: Tafalla (Navarre, February), Salamanca (April), also in this month at Mairena del Alcor (Seville) and Jerez de la Frontera; in May, there is a Carnation Show in Sitges; in June, a rounding-up, branding and sale of wild horses at Mougas (Pontevedra); in September, at Reinosa (Santander), one of the most important horse shows in northern Spain; in November, there are important livestock fairs at Huesca, Leon and Ciudad Rodrigo.

CARNIVALS

Carnivals are not a feature of Spanish life, but they are observed in Las Palmas, Santa Cruz and Orotava (all in the Canaries), where the three days ending with Ash Wednesday are devoted to feasting and merrymaking. Men and women parade the streets, masked and dressed in fancy costumes. Confetti, paper ribbons, etc., are thrown and the population takes part in various amusements. At Arrecife, capital of the island of Lanzarote, the carnival is celebrated rather strangely. The men dress up in women's clothes, blacken their faces, and run through the streets indulging in a gibbering language. It is all very odd and amusing.

CULTURAL EVENTS

The most important musical festival held in Spain is the **International Festival of Music and Dance** held in Granada, usually during the last ten days in June. In this historic city, with its mysterious and hauntingly beautiful palace of the Alhambra whose patios provide unforgettable settings for chamber music; with its palace built by Charles V where open-air orchestral concerts are given; with the famous nearby gardens of the Generalife used for enchanting ballet productions, this is an event which is sure to delight.

Santander also puts on an **International Festival of Music and Dance,** during the last week in August. Seville, too, has its **Music Festival** about the end of September and early October; also San Sebastian (July), which also provides a **Film Festival** during the same period. Worth noting is the **Festival of Mediterranean Song** held in Barcelona at the end of September.

If you happen to be in Madrid during the summer, it is pleasant to visit the outdoor theatre in the Retiro Park, where performances of **ballet** are often given amidst a setting of trees, with possibly a moon, when the scene is a fairyland. There is also a marionette theatre for children.

To many tourists Spain is primarily the land of **flamenco dancing** and **bullfights.** Many night-clubs stage the former. An excellent place to see these colourful dances is the Hotel Maria Cristina in Seville, for it is here that promising performers are given the opportunity to show their skill. The Casino can also be recommended for this typical entertainment. In Madrid, there is the expensive Zambra and the bohemian Casablanca (men only), while in Barcelona the liveliest spot is El Cortijo. The gypsy flamenco dancing in Granada always seems to me to be a sheer tourist racket; but in Valencia, the Terraza Jardin Rialto is first-class.

NATIONAL OR SPECIAL DAYS

On July 18th there are country-wide celebrations commemorating the beginning of the existing Franco regime.

Commemoration of the Reconquest of Granada, January 2nd, Granada. This is celebrated by a civic-religious procession, with Mass in the Cathedral; the occasion has been carried on ever since 1492.

Commemoration of the Incorporation of Gran' Canary in the Kingdom of Castile, January 29th, Las Palmas. Procession bearing the banner of the Conquest. Local-style wrestling, cock fighting, folklore events, flower and bird shows, etc. This Feast of San Pedro de Verona, as it is known, dates back to 1483.

RELIGIOUS EVENTS

Holy Week* (*Semana Santa*) in Spain is possibly the outstanding religious celebration held not only in Spain but in Europe. But you must

Funchal, Madeira   *Firework Display*

Fatima, Portugal   *Pilgrimage*

Patras, Greece   *Carnival Dancing*

Valencia, Spain   *The Fallas*

be prepared to go to see it in the right frame of mind, and with no critical, carping attitude. For the days, the week prior to Easter, commemorating Christ's Passion and Death are days of deep and, in a way, surprisingly sincere mourning for Spaniards of every class and condition. As a people they are, like the Russians, fascinated by the idea of suffering and death—not as a rule morbidly so, but as a theme which makes them even more intensely aware of their own aliveness, and of the imperative need to enjoy life to the full—a characteristic, by the way, which is also un-mistakeably revealed by the bullfight.

Briefly, Holy Week is celebrated by the processions of various religious brotherhoods, each belonging to a church and each one illustrating a scene from the Passion. Lighted by hundreds of candles and surrounded by flowers, the *pasos*, or religious floats, are carried very slowly on the backs of 25 or 30 bearers, followed by the brotherhood members dressed in long pointed black or white hoods and going barefooted. Some of the *pasos* are beautifully made by famous artists of the past, and nearly all bring home the idea of intense human suffering in a way which may shock Nordic susceptibilities. The streets are blacked out, and the only sound is the occasional tolling of the church bells for the dead, and the nerve-tightening beat of a single drum, which sets the slow pace for these hooded figures, moving stiffly in unison, as though part of some fantastic nightmare. Frequent halts have to be made to allow the bearers of the heavy *paso* to rest, often to swill some wine, so that in some cases they become intoxicated. It is during one or other of these halts that the *saetas*, those weird songs and impromptu laments, rend the air, to say nothing of your heart. The scene is certainly one you will never forget, but although Seville is the most famous city for its Holy Week ceremonies, because of the magnificence of the various religious fraternities that file through the streets, hour after hour throughout the night, I feel the event has become rather too commercialised for the visitor, and I would prefer to recommend some other place, outstanding centres being Malaga, Murcia, Toledo, Cuenca, Granada, Zamora and Valladolid.

Between noon of Thursday and midnight on Friday, all traffic and public services are reduced to a minimum, while many people wear only black, so ladies especially should bear this in mind. Strangely enough, on Saturday, all mourning is set aside and celebrations in general are the order of the day. Seeing that Christ is not supposed to have risen until midnight on this day, the Spanish attitude may seem surprising—but you must just accept it. Remember, too, that prior booking at hotels is essential, and be prepared for considerably higher prices (authorised).

Passion Plays are featured in certain Catalonian towns, including Olesa (near Barcelona) which is the best and is performed every Sunday and feast day during Lent; it dates from 1642, and the townsfolk take

K

the various parts.   Molins de Rey (on the road to Montserrat) and Cervera (between Barcelona and Lerida) are two more suggestions.

Next to Holy Week, the **Feast of Corpus Christi*** is next in importance. It is celebrated with pomp and processions in many parts of Spain. Once again enormous *pasos* are carried through the streets, and in some cases they are accompanied by *seizes*—small boys dressed in medieval garments, who have the age-old privilege of scattering flower petals before the Sacred Host during the procession. In Seville Cathedral these choristers actually dance before the altar, wearing plumed hats and dresses of the time of Philip III, red and white for Corpus Christi, and blue and white for the Virgin (Feast of the Assumption—August 15th). Another special custom observed on the occasion of this feast, at Sitges and at Orotava (Canaries), is the carpeting of streets with flowers, arranged in beautiful designs. Granada is the best place for this festival, and during the period various cultural attractions are presented, among them the class cal *Autos Sacramentales*, acted on a stage in the courtyard of the cathedral. But in all communities there are entertainments, including bull-fights and fireworks. Toledo, Cadiz and Seville are other recommendations for festivities.

It is impossible to detail all the interesting religious festivals in Spain, for every city and village celebrates its patron saint, but the following six events merit special mention:

Festival of San Isidro (May 15th) is an important occasion, for he is linked with many towns, including Leon, Madrid and Alicante. In the capital of Spain there are many artistic, cultural and sporting events, regional dances, bullfights, etc., during the period. Leon, with its superb cathedral, is another exciting goal, even though the local hotel accommodation is merely adequate.

Romeria of El Rocio, Whitsunday. A *romeria* is a kind of picnic excursion to a shrine, usually on horseback or in ox-wagons. In the case of El Rocio, this is the most famous and picturesque of all Spain's " romerias." The pilgrims come to pay their respects to the miraculous Virgin of El Rocio, not far from Almonte. The pilgrims, who come from all over Andalusia, spend most of the nights around camp-fires, singing and making love to the sound of their guitars. They travel mostly in garlanded carts and wear typical pilgrim's costume of the region.

Human Towers, St. John's Day (June 24th). Another unusual celebration on this day is the *Xiquets de Valls*, or the human towers of Valls. This is a gymnastic feat which has come down through the centuries, and it comprises a tower of men, six at the base and six men high. This feat can be seen at other places, too, notably at nearby Tarragona, Reus and Montblanch.

Festival of St. James the Apostle,* July 23rd to 30th, Santiago de Compostela. St. James is the patron saint of Spain, and his day is celebrated each year with brilliant pomp in that wonderful Galician city, where his remains are said to be buried in the great cathedral. On the eve of St. James's Day (July 24th) there are fireworks in the great square outside the cathedral. On July 25th, a glittering procession follows the Archbishop, dressed in silver, up the nave. During the service the famous seven-foot censer swings across the central arm of the transept, almost touching the ceiling—quite an alarming sight. But, for me, pride of place in this lovely building is the three-arched Portico de la Gloria, one of the finest masterpieces of stone carving in Spain. Accompanying the festival is a variety of entertainments, some of them extremely noisy. But it is an event well worth making a special trip.

Mystery of Elche, August 14th-15th, Elche. This little town, inland from Alicante, is unique for several reasons. It possesses the only palm forest in Europe, and it supplies the whole country with palm branches to be blessed on Palm Sunday. It is the site where the famous statue, " The Lady of Elche," was found, believed to be 3,000 years old, and now to be seen in the Prado Museum in Madrid. Lastly, and most important, in the Church of la Merced every year representations of an unchanged 13th century musical miracle play are given. I must warn you, however, that in mid-August the heat in Elche can be sizzling.

Festival of Our Lady of the Pillar, October 12th, Zaragoza. Just 40 years after the birth of Christ, during Saint James's missionary trip through Spain, Our Lady appeared to him on a sacred pillar and told him to build a church on the spot. The church has now become a great cathedral, but the pillar is still there, and thousands of pilgrims come on the anniversary of the Virgin's appearance to pay homage to it and the blackened figure of the Virgin in the sanctuary. In addition to the religious observances, this festival includes a folklore rally, giants and dwarfs, fireworks, musical competitions, bullfights, etc.

Some other special festivals are tabulated as follows:

Cavalcade of the " Three Wise Men From the East," Las Palmas, January 5th. Also elsewhere in Spain.

" Three Wise Men of the East " (religious play), Aledo, Murcia, January 6th.

St. Anthony's Day, Gallegos del Pan, Puebla de Hijar, Benicasm, Orrellana, Manacor, in January. At Gallegos del Pan there are typical plays, with feasting and dancing in the local wine vaults.

St. Sebastian's Day, Huelva, San Sebastian, Sotillo de las Palomas, Pollensa, January.

" The Holy Mystery," Cervera, February 6th. A play commemorating a miracle that took place in 1540.

" La Passio," Cervera, Molins de Rey, Esparraguera, Olesa de Montserrat, First Sunday in Lent and every Sunday during Lent and during Holy Week. A religious play.

Feast of St. Tecla, Tarragona, September 23rd.

Two curious religious celebrations are those which take place at La Puebla del Caramiñal (Galicia) and at Valverde (Canaries). In the former instance, each year on the third Sunday of September it is the custom for persons who have been dangerously ill during the previous 12 months to proceed in procession to the church, each one following an empty coffin—to be used later, by the way. At Valverde, every fourth year, early in May, the image of the Virgin de los Reyes is brought from the Ermita de los Reyes across the island to Valverde and carried back at the end of nine days. On each occasion it is accompanied by a number of dancers (*bailarines*), who, like David before the ark, dance the whole time. Then, during the statue's sojourn in Valverde, any man on payment of a small fee is allowed to carry the Virgin in his arms for a short stroll along the main street. This is called " taking the Virgin for a *paseo*." A *paseo*, incidentally, is the evening stroll to be seen in every Spanish town.

PILGRIMAGES

The six most important places of pilgrimages in Spain are:

Guadalupe. This is the most beautiful, inspiring and lovable shrine in Spain; but it is rather difficult to reach, except by car. It is 55 miles east of Trujillo. The convent is an excellent specimen of Mauresque art, the cloisters very peaceful, and the Chapel contains the " Virgin of Guadalupe," said to have been carved by St. Luke. The treasury is incredibly rich and is said to contain the finest collection of vestments in existence. The church possesses eight of Zurbaran's paintings. In 1928, Our Lady of Guadalupe was proclaimed Queen of Spain. The most important day of pilgrimage is October 12th.

Santiago. Elsewhere in this chapter I have mentioned this art town. The chief time of pilgrimage is on Saint James's Day (July 25th).

Montserrat. This monastery is situated on a Holy Mountain, easily reached from Barcelona. In the church is the much-venerated statue of the Virgin—the Black Virgin—said to have been carved by St. Luke and brought to Spain by St. Peter. There is a school of ecclesiastical music run by the Benedictine monks, held to be the oldest in Europe; and the singing of the choir is a musical treat which should not be missed. The chief pilgrimage is on April 27th (Day of the Virgin).

Covadonga. In the middle of the maze of mountains of Asturias is the cave where Don Pelayo and his handful of knights lived when they sallied forth to fight the first battle against the Moors, opening a struggle in 718 which was to last for eight centuries. It was in this cave that Pelayo found the miraculous image (very popular in Spain), and the spot has now been turned into a chapel. Nearby is a 19th century church, standing on an imposing site. The main occasion of pilgrimage is on September 8th.

Almonte. Described elsewhere as the goal of Spain's most important " romeria," this is the shrine of the miraculous Virgin of El Rocio. The chief date of pilgrimage is Whitsunday.

Cabeza. Tucked away in the Sierra Morena, this picturesque mountainous spot is 20 miles from the nearest town, Andujar. Dating from the 13th century, this shrine to the Holy Virgin came into special prominence during the Civil War, when there was fierce fighting in the vicinity, with a strong resistance offered by the Nationalist garrison. Because of this historic incident, the popularity of the Virgin of Cabeza has increased tremendously, and the " romeria " in her honour which is held each year at the end of April is one of the most important in Spain.

SPORTING FIXTURES

Association football is extremely popular in Spain, and the climax comes in Madrid towards the end of June when the **Generalissimo's Cup** is competed for.

The **Grand Prix,** a motor-car race held in Barcelona, takes place at the end of October. It contributes points to the world championship.

There is a **Tour of Spain** for cyclists at the end of May and early June. Horse racing in Madrid (early September to November), and in San Sebastian (from mid-July). This seaside resort also holds an **International Horse Show** during late July. The main yachting regattas are at Santander (summer) and at Malaga (January). There are similar events at other ports around the Spanish coast.

The typical Basque game of pelota is played by professionals in Madrid, Barcelona, Palma de Mallorca, Bilbao, Zaragoza, San Sebastian and Pamplona. It is an extremely fast and thrilling game, with considerable opportunities for betting. In Madrid, there are nightly matches between women players, but they lack the skill and strength of the men professionals. In the northern Basque country the game is played throughout the summer, and championship contests are usually held in one of the centres around the end of August.

Pigeon-shooting is a popular sport in Spain, and there are competitions during the year at a number of Spanish towns, including Madrid, Malaga, San Sebastian and Valencia.

BULLFIGHTS

Almost every visitor to Spain wants to see at least one bullfight. Actually, it is a ritual as well as a sport. You may disapprove of it; you may oppose it; but you cannot ignore it. And if, as a Briton, you condemn it on terms of cruelty, I would remind you that in Spain they have no Society for the Prevention of Cruelty to Children—because it is not needed—while in Britain we hold an unenviable lead in this connection.

I am not going to describe bull-fighting, and if you are really interested in this typical Spanish entertainment I suggest you buy a copy of " Bulls and Bullfighting," by J. L. Acquaroni (Editorial Noguer, Barcelona), which is available in an English edition.

Briefly then I would state that most Spanish festivals include a bull-fight as a star performance, while in cities, such as Madrid and Barcelona, there are regular weekly *corridas*, usually on Sundays from Easter until the end of November. Famous bullfighters, by the way, are adored in Spain, and when they die their tombs often become shrines of pilgrimage.

A distinctly curious bullfight takes place in Pamplona,* the capital of Navarre, during the **Festival of San Fermin** (July 7th). In this festival, bulls intended for the *corrida* are allowed to run loose through the streets of the town, while the young " bloods " rush out with capes to keep them on their course. The less courageous occupy balconies and cheer the volunteer matadors. It is an amusing spectacle, accompanied sometimes by danger. There are other festivities on this occasion. As accommodation in Pamplona may be strained at this festival time (including increased prices), I suggest that as San Sebastian is only 60 miles away, most people may prefer to stay there and go to Pamplona on excursion.

For those interested to see the training of bulls for fighting purposes, there are opportunities in the neighbourhood of Salamanca, but the most important training-grounds are around Seville and Cordoba.

TRADE FAIRS
Samples Fair, Valencia, early May.
Samples Fair, Barcelona, early June.
Samples Fair, Bilbao, August.

TRADITIONAL CUSTOMS
Many traditional festivals have a religious background and as they are so numerous I list the more important and interesting ones month by month; but check up on the exact dates, for they often vary from year to year.

January
Malaga. Winter Festival, with golf, tennis, horse-riding competitions, regattas, pigeon shooting, opera, displays of regional folk-dancing.
Alicante. Winter Festival. Pigeon-shooting, racing, regatta.

February
Cadiz Grand folklore festival, cavalcade of over 3,000 masked figures, decorated ox-carts, bands, choirs and pageants; battle of flowers.

Caceres. Candlemas. Women wear traditional "campuza" costumes.

Zamora. Festival of the "Aguedas." Girls, wearing regional costumes, pass through the streets, dancing local folk-dances.

Toro (Zamora). Carnival dances with typical regional dresses, including the famous one known as the "Rich Widow."

March

Valencia. "Fallas" of St. Joseph.* This is probably the noisiest festivity in Europe, and it lasts a week. The "fallas" are grotesque effigies of men, women and animals, often with a satirical slant. Some are veritable works of art, but apart from the first prize winning exhibit the remainder are set on fire around midnight on St. Joseph's Day (March 19th). But, for safety's sake, no "falla" can be set on fire until a fire-engine is in attendance. In addition, there are fireworks, bands, and all the fun of a fair. This is certainly a festival to be seen once in a lifetime.

Murcia. Spring Festival, including the "Burial of the Sardine." For several days, there are lively parades, battles of flowers, bullfights, and displays of regional costumes. The "Burial of the Sardine" takes place, under the light of torches, around midnight. Its origin is vague, but it is thought to be the burial of Winter and the rebirth of Adonis, personification of Spring.

April

La Alberga (Salamanca). *Corridas de gallos en cabellerias.* Richly dressed riders, passing at full gallop, compete to catch cocks suspended over their heads.

Alcoy. Traditional festivities in honour of St. George. A mock battle is staged between the "Moors" and the "Christians," including the dummy capture of a castle and much noise. Bullfights.

Seville. Spring Fair.* This is the most important festival in Spain, and it follows about a fortnight after Easter. Open booths, called "casetas," are erected along the street, where families and clubs receive their friends and offer refreshments and entertainments in the form of flamenco dancing and singing to the accompaniment of guitars. Every day there is a first-class bullfight, along with parades of gaily decorated carriages with fine horses and costumed *señoritas* wearing the old-time white mantillas with gorgeous shawls and jewels. You will see nowhere else in the world such beautiful women. As for Holy Week, hotel accommodation must be booked months in advance, while prices are doubled, including hotel rates, bullfights ticket, taxis and carriages. And whether you stay for a day or a week, you must pay for the week.

Jerez de la Frontera. Spring Fair and Festival, mostly around the first three days of May. Parades, regional dancing, bullfights, etc.

May

Lerida. St. Anastasius Festival. Giants' and dwarfs' procession, various local regional customs, including " marraco," " ball de bastons," and " sardanas." Folk-dancing competitions, sports, etc.

Soller (Majorca). Mock battle between " Moors " and " Christians," commemorating an historic feat of arms.

Ronda. Festival commemorating the reconquest of the town by the Catholic Kings. Bullfights and fair, etc.

Aranjuez and **La Granja.** Magnificent fountains play in the gardens on certain dates. Enquire from Tourist Office in Madrid regarding dates and times.

June

La Laguna (Tenerife). Feast of St. Benedict. Folklore rally, local-style wrestling, parade of garlanded carts, etc.

Cordova. Fair and Festival of Nuestra Senora de la Salud, including processions, regional dancing, bullfights, etc.

Alicante. Popular " St. John's Bonfires," with the setting up and burning of artistic groups of figures in wood and cardboard. Bullfights.

San Pedro Manrique (Soria). Festival of reparation in honour of the " mondidas " damsels, by purification by fire. On midsummer night young men pass barefoot over a bonfire, carrying another person on their backs.

Ciudadela (Minorca). Feast of St. John. Typical cavalcade of richly caparisoned horses, with riders in period costumes. In addition to jousts, the horsemen urge their steeds up staircases and into the living-rooms of the people, who pelt them with nuts and lighted fireworks.

Segovia. Feast of St. John. Dancing with regional dresses.

Leon. St. John's Fair. Bullfights, bowling and wrestling tournaments.

Burgos. St. Peter's Fair and Festival. Parades, regional dances, bullfights, etc. Typical Castilian " romeria."

Lequeitio (Biscay). Feast of St. Peter. Festivities organised by the Fishermen's Confraternity. Unique, symbolic dance, the " kasharanra," performed by a man on the ancient coffer of the guild, supported on the shoulders of four sailors.

Irun. Feast of St. Martial. Typical " alarde " commemorative parade.

July

Seo de Urgel. Festival of St. Odon. " Ball cerda " dance, in which the performers wear rich and colourful regional costumes.

Puerto de la Cruz (Tenerife). Festival in honour of the " Gran Poder de Dios " and Our Lady of Mt. Carmel. Popular celebrations, folk-dances and songs. Canary-style wrestling, etc.

Roncal (Navarre). Traditional tribute of three cows offered by farmers in the French valleys to those in the Spanish.

Santa Cruz de Tenerife. Festival of Our Lady of Carmel. Parade, folklore rally, Canary-style wrestling, popular festivities.

Bailen (Jaen). Patriotic festival commemorating the Battle of Bailen. Pageant announcing the festivities led by a cavalcade of representative figures in period costume. Tribute to the women of Bailen. Civic-religious procession to the battle-field.

Tafalla (Navarre). Typical festival. Dawn Confraternity procession. Dancing in the streets, bullfights, rounding-up of bulls.

Betanzos (Corunna). St. Roch Fair. Interesting dances by farm-workers and sailors' guilds, " caneiros," etc.

Tarragona. St. Magin Festival. Giants and dwarfs. Symbolic carrying of water from the shrine of St. Magin de Bruhfagana to Tarragona.

Castro-Urdiales (Santander). " Coso Blanco " festival. Parade of garlanded farm-carts, battle of flowers, regatta, bullfights.

Montehermoso (Caceres). Feast of St. Bartholomew. " Romeria " in which all the people wear traditional regional dress. Dances and songs.

Arrecife (Canaries). St. Gines Festival. Sporting events, including Canary-style wrestling.

Corunna. Bagpipe contests, regional dances, " romeria," decorated farm-carts, etc.

Torremolinos. Fair and " romeria."

Bilbao. " Semana Grande," with various types of festivities, including bullfights.

Santander. Feast of St. James. Festivities begin with a cavalcade. Regional dances, folklore exhibitions, bullfights, etc. During this period the International Festival of Theatre, Dance and Music is usually held.

Villafranca de Oria (Guipuzcoa). Feast of St. Anne. Traditional " auresku " dance by men married during preceding year.

La Laguna (Tenerife). Banner taken from the Town Hall to the Cathedral, with religious procession.

Valldemosa (Majorca). Feast of St. Catalina Thomas. Unique celebrations, including folklore performance of Majorcan " El Parado de Valldemosa " song and dance.

Valencia. Festival of St. James, with battle of flowers, musical competitions, bullfights, etc.

August

Huelva. Columbus Festival, commemorating the departure of Columbus from the Port of Palos on his voyage of discovery. Sports, typical costumes, bullfights.

Pollensa (Majorca). " Moors and Christians " Festival.

Palma de Mallorca. Pageant representing the entry of St. Catalina Thomas into the city, surrounded by her choir of singing angels.

Ibiza. Commemoration of the Reconquest of the Island by the Christians in 1235.

Corunna. "Semana Grande." Maria Pita Festival. Bullfights, sports, etc.

Guetaria (Guipuzcoa). Traditional pageant commemorating the landing of Juan Sebastian Elcano after his first voyage round the world.

Malaga. Anniversary of the reconquest of the city by the Catholic Kings. Fair and festival, bullfights, sports meetings, folklore rallies, parades, etc.

Huesca. St. Lawrence's Fair. Traditional procession with dancers. Bullfights. " Jota " and Aragonese folklore festival.

El Escorial. Feast of St. Lawrence. Fair, bullfights, etc.

Pontevedra. Fifteen-day " Peregrina " Festival. Folk-dancing, bullfights, battles of flowers.

San Sebastian. "Semana Grande." Regattas, sports meetings, music and folklore festival, bullfights, etc.

Candelaria (Tenerife). Feast of the Patron Saint of the island, in which masked shepherds perform an appearance of Our Lady to the native islanders.

Leon. Festival celebrated in the cathedral, commemorating the tribute of 100 damsels given by the Kings of Leon to the Moors until the battle of Clavijo. Traditional costumes.

September

Sarinena (Huesca). Feast of St. Antolin. Typical dances, and performance of " dichos," with simulated medieval fight.

Barco de Avila (Avila). Procession of the Swallows, in which these birds invariably circle round the statue of Christ.

Palencia. Feast of St. Antolin. Folklore Festival.

Cuenca. St. Julian's Fair. This fascinating town can be reached by day-excursion from Madrid, for hotel accommodation is limited.

Aranjuez. Fair and Festival. Fountains play in the gardens.

Mahon (Minorca). " La Colcada " Festival.

Ronda. Fair and Festival. Bullfights, flamenco singing competition. Dances with regional dresses. Livestock fair.

El Escorial. " Romeria." Dance and dress competitions. Parade of decorated ox-carts.

Villarejo del Valle (Avila). The most important " vitor " in the province. Colourful cavalcade with regional dresses.

Aldea de San Nicholas (Grand Canary). " Charco " festival. Local inhabitants go to the Charco lagoon, into which, on a given signal, they dive and catch fish bred there since the year before.

Cuenca. Festival commemorating the reconquest of the city by Alphonso VIII. Civic procession. Fighting with heifers, etc.

Oviedo. St. Matthew's Fair. Sports festival, " America in Asturias " Day. Parades, bullfights.

Tarragona. Festival of St. Tecla. Folklore rally, " sardanas," " xiquets " (human towers), bullfights, etc.

Barcelona. Festival of Our Lady of Ransom. Bullfights, folklore, " sardanas," dances, etc.

Cordova. Autumn Fair. Typical parades, dancing, bullfights.

Icod de Los Vinos (Tenerife). Festival in honour of the " Santissimo Cristo del Calvario." Artistic function at the foot of the thousand-year-old dragon-tree, with girls symbolically dressed to represent the Hispano-American republics.

Salamanca. Fair and Festival, with bullfights, etc.

October

Lugo. Festival of St. Froilan. Traditional costumes and dances. River regatta, " verbenas," parades.

Avila. Special offering to the " Virgen de Sonsoles " by the people of the region, many dressed in traditional costumes. Traditional " juego de la bandera " (flag-play).

Jaen. St. Luke's Fair. Bullfights, dancing, etc.

Arenas de San Pedro (Avila). A " romeria," with couples riding two-up, in the traditional manner, to the monastery founded by St. Peter of Alcantara.

Seville. Michaelmas Fair and Festival, with processions, bullfights, etc.

November

Medinaceli (Soria). " Cuerpos Santos " festival. Midnight procession. Traditional " jubillo " (fighting a bull at night, the animal's horns being tipped with balls of burning pitch and resin). Typical regional costumes.

December

Torrejoncillo (Caceres). " La Encamisada." Traditional festival with procession in which riders draped in sheets accompany the Virgin. Regional dances.

Palma de Mallorca. Festival commemorating the reconquest of Palma.

WINE FESTIVALS

During the second week of September, the famous sherry town of Jerez de la Frontera holds its **Vintage Feast.** There is a blessing of the grapes, various competitions and bullfights.

Logroño, centre of the largest wine-growing district of Spain also holds a **Vintage Festival** about the third week in September.

CHAPTER TWENTY-FIVE

Sweden

THE MONTH OF MIDSUMMER IS UNDOUBTEDLY ONE OF THE FINEST periods to visit Sweden. Nature is at her best; in the south, night barely encroaches on long June days, while in the north the sun never sets at all. And the Swedes, each one of them a sun-worshipper at heart, are in festive mood.

This is the month when the Stockholm Festival draws opera, ballet and music lovers from all over the world, and the city is at her loveliest. It is the month, too, when all Swedes rejoice at midsummer with all-night festivities. Earlier, on June 6th, National Day celebrations take place.

CULTURAL EVENTS

Stockholm Festival, Stockholm, first two weeks of June. This is perhaps the greatest of the four big Scandinavian cultural festivals. The programme includes opera, ballet, music and drama, all of it excellent; but the highlight, surely, is provided by the opera performances in the superb setting of Drottningholm Court Theatre in its lovely gardens. For these performances, the original 18th century settings and stage machinery are used, and you can first set your mood by a 40-minute steamer trip to the theatre from the city centre through the soft daylight of the northern evening, and the great panorama of lakes and forests. The Festival is also the occasion of much festivity, including the election of the Queen of Mälaren in front of the city's distinctive Town Hall, attended by water ski-ing displays and a salute of guns from naval boats gathered in the harbour for the event.

Petrus de Dacia, Visby, several performances in July. This music drama, based on the life of a 13th century Swedish Dominican monk, is staged against the background of the ruined St. Nicholas monastery.

The Road to Heaven, Leksand, second half of July. A morality play which captures the spirit of old Dalecarlia province and presents Biblical events as the villagers of the past imagined them unfolding in their own surroundings. The play is performed in a natural amphi-theatre—and it's interesting to note that, since its revival nearly 30 years ago, only one performance has been cancelled due to bad weather !

Nobel Prize-Giving Ceremony, Stockholm, December 10th.

Awards to those who have contributed most to the common good in the fields of chemistry, physics, medicine, literature and peace are made each year from the income of a trust fund established by the Swedish scientist, Alfred Nobel, who died on this day in 1896. The Peace Prize is awarded in Oslo.

NATIONAL OR SPECIAL DAYS

Walpurgis Night, all over the country, April 30th. All Swedes welcome the return of spring with bonfires, but the students especially have made this their celebration day and festivities reach their peak in the university towns of Uppsala and Lund. It's an evening, too, for parties and all-night revelry.

National Day, all over the country, June 6th. The blue and yellow of Sweden's flag flutters everywhere on this day. Parades and speeches take place in Stockholm Stadium before the King, who presents silken flags to various organisations and popular movements.

Midsummer Eve, all over the country, week-end nearest to June 23rd. This is the time to head into the Swedish countryside—to the villages, big and small, where maypoles entwined with birch leaves provide the focal point of festivities. On jetties and in barns, folk music and dancing continue through a night which only briefly interrupts the long midsummer days in southern Sweden. The best centre in Stockholm is Skansen Park; outside the capital, try and make for Dalecarlia province where, at Leksand, thousands gather to watch the race between " church " boats, once used to carry whole villages to Sunday worship. Special coach tours enable you to visit several centres on this evening when all Sweden rejoices in the sun.

SPORTING FIXTURES

Vasa Ski Race, Sälen-Mora, first Sunday in March. In 1521, King Gustav Vasa did this 50-mile course on skis in the opposite direction, trying to whip up enthusiasm for his cause against the Danish invaders. He was eventually successful, and today this cross-country race has become Sweden's big spring ski-ing event. Anyone can take part, and it presents an astonishing scene as well over 1,000 skiers of all ages and descriptions hasten across the snow towards the finishing post at Mora, popular tourist centre in the heart of Dalecarlia province.

Stånga Games, Isle of Gotland, during first week of July. Traditional local games have been played in this way for centuries. Events include a rodeo, in which children ride tough Gotland ponies bare-back.

TRADE FAIRS

Swedish Industries Fair, Gothenburg, during last two weeks of May.

St. Erik's Fair, Stockholm, late August or early September. An international trade fair, amongst the biggest in Europe.

Scandinavian Design Cavalcade, mainly in Stockholm, September. Swedish arts, crafts and industrial design on show in exhibitions and window displays.

TRADITIONAL CUSTOMS

Lapp Fair, Jokkmokk, early February. Biggest of the Swedish Lapp winter fairs, dominated by the sale of game and skins, this is also a great folk feast and religious festival, particularly amongst the Laestadius Sect of the Lutheran Church. Lapps from the remotest homesteads flock into town to trade and celebrate.

Lapp Fair, Gällivare, end of March or early April. Lapps from all over northern Sweden trade in reindeer, sell their handicrafts, get married and have their children christened.

St. Lucia's Day, all over the country, December 13th. This essentially Swedish festival, paying homage to the patron saint of Light during the days of northern winter darkness, has borrowed a Sicilian martyr as its central character. In every home, St. Lucia is personified by a girl, usually the eldest daughter, dressed in white with a crown of lighted candles on her head, who serves coffee and special saffron cakes to the rest of the family. Nowadays, too, every town elects its own Lucia, the biggest celebration taking place in Stockholm, where a parade of the elected one, with her attendants and gaily decorated carriages, culminates in a banquet at the City Hall.

CHAPTER TWENTY-SIX

Switzerland

SUCH IS THE VARIETY OF MOOD, BOTH IN LANDSCAPE AND entertainment, that almost any time is the " best " time to visit Switzerland. With its three main languages (German, French, Italian), its two principal religions (Roman Catholicism and Protestantism), and its two distinctly separate tourist seasons (winter sports, and the rest), the range of choice packed into such a small country must be almost unbeatable, so that you can go at any time and be sure of finding some unusual and worthwhile event.

If you want to see the Alpine flowers at their loveliest, however, I strongly recommend June—a glorious time in the mountains and an excellent month, too, for cultural activities in Lausanne and Zurich.

Of the many traditional events, the Landsgemeinde, one of the Open Air Parliaments held at the end of April or early in May in some cantons, is particularly worth seeing. Amongst the carnivals, Basle's " Fasnacht " is certainly the loudest and the jolliest. For nation-wide celebrations of a more sober nature, the National Day on August 1st will always remain very close to the heart of every Swiss.

AGRICULTURAL, HORTICULTURAL AND LIVESTOCK SHOWS

Rose Weeks, Geneva, June. For two weeks, Geneva becomes a city of roses, including illuminated rose gardens and international " new rose " competitions.

Olma Swiss Farm and Dairy Fair, St. Gall, ten days in October.

CARNIVALS

Maidens' Sunday, Fahrwangen and Meisterschwanden (Seetal, Aargau), second Sunday in January. In honour of the women of both Communes with a great fancy dress procession.

Vogel Gryff, Basle, January 13th, 20th or 27th depending on which Company presides over the Ceremony. In this Festival of the three " Companies of Honour " of Lesser Basle dance through the streets. At the inaugural ceremony the " Wild Man," accompanied by drummers and standard-bearers, sails down the Rhine on a raft to the middle bridge, where he is welcomed by " Vogel Gryff " (the Griffin) and the Lion.

Shrovetide Carnivals. Starting with " Schmutzig " Thursday, the Thursday before Ash Wednesday, it's carnival time in most of the Catholic parts of Switzerland. " Schmutzig " or " Fat " Thursday, so called because of the pancakes eaten at this time, is the main day in Brunnen when masked **Bartli** parades through the town, and Lucerne holds its **Fritschi** procession.

On the Sunday, the **Rollelibutzen** dance through the streets of Altstätten, near St. Gall; on the Monday there's a " Tyrolean " masked dance at Rothenthurm in Schwyz, while **Gretschell** is the central masked character to appear in Zug.

On Shrove Tuesday, the people of Lugano and other towns in Ticino, Switzerland's southern province, enjoy a risotto meal in the main squares. Finally, on Ash Wednesday, the incarnation of the carnival spirit receives a satirical burial at Herisau.

Fasnacht, Basle Carnival,* Basle, Monday and Wednesday after Ash Wednesday. Early risers will appreciate this event which opens with a noisy procession of drumming clubs at four o'clock in the morning ! Festivities continue with masked parades through the decorated streets, and masked balls far into the night.

Festival of Flowers and Grand Procession, Locarno, Whit Sunday and Monday.

Grand Evening Lakeside Festival, Lucerne, early July.

Geneva Festival, Geneva, second or third week-end in August. Battle of flowers, fancy dress parade, confetti fights, firework display and open air balls.

CULTURAL EVENTS

Son et Lumière, Sion, end of April to September. An outstanding performance on the slopes above this picturesque town, against the backdrop of the ruined castle.

Lausanne International Festival, Lausanne, from end of May or early June. Opera, ballet, music and drama.

June Arts Festival, Zurich, June. Music, opera, ballet, drama, exhibitions.

William Tell Open Air Plays, Interlaken, mid-July to end of August. The story of the legendary Tell and his fight to free his country from Austrian rule unfolds against a rural background.

Locarno International Film Festival, Locarno, July.

International Festival of Music, Lucerne, mid-August to early September. An excellent programme includes performances in the open air by the famous Lion Monument.

Yehudi Menuhin Festival, Gstaad, end of August.

Ascona Music Festival, Ascona, end of August to October.

Musical September of Montreux, Montreux, September.

Dubrovnik, Yugoslavia   *" Hamlet "*

tend, Belgium   *Blessing of the Sea*   Arezzo, Italy   *Joust of the Saracens*

Interlaken, Switzerland *William Tell Play*

Seville, Spain *Holy Week* Visby, Sweden *Midsummer Ni*

Organ Recitals,* Fribourg Cathedral, regularly during the summer. Outstanding performances in architecturally splendid surroundings. I count these amongst the highlights of my musical experiences in Europe.

Choral Festivals. Every village has its choral society and each region holds its festival, usually of a high standard, at regular intervals. A Federal Choral Festival provides the climax of these activities.

NATIONAL OR SPECIAL DAYS

National Day, all over the country, August 1st. On this day in 1291, the men of Uri, Schwyz and Unterwalden concluded a " Perpetual Pact " on the meadow of Rütli, Lake Lucerne, to fight for their rights against their Hapsburg overlords. It was to provide the first step towards an independent Swiss Confederation. To honour this day, bells ring across city, village, lake and mountain pasture, and the night glows with thousands of bonfires, scene of rousing music and patriotic speeches.

RELIGIOUS EVENTS

Sacred Processions, Mendrisio, near Lugano, Maundy Thursday and Good Friday. The journey to Golgotha is re-enacted in an impressive procession on the Thursday, followed by torchlight processions on Good Friday.

Corpus Christi Processions, in many Catholic districts, but particularly at Appenzell, Bulle, Einsiedeln, Fribourg, Lucerne, Sion, Wil, on the Thursday ten days after Whitsun. Probably the most impressive of these is at Fribourg, where the streets are bedecked with Gobelins and other costly tapestries.

Ascension Day Ride, Beromunster. The clergy and canons in their brightly coloured coats ride round the diocese on horseback with a solemn entry into the town.

Benediction Sunday, Lötschental, Sunday following Corpus Christi. The parade of the Lord's Grenadiers in their colourful traditional uniforms provides the main feature of this festival at Blatten and Kippel, against the backdrop of a peaceful Alpine valley.

The Great World Theatre,* Einsiedeln, June to September, every five years. Six representatives of humanity, from beggar to king, face the tests of life's problems and must account for their deeds on the Day of Judgement. This very moving play unfolds before the monastery church, and was last performed in 1960.

Engelweihe, Religious Festival, Einsiedeln, September 14th. A great torchlight procession in the Monastery Square, dominated by a huge altar ablaze with light.

SPORTING FIXTURES

Winter Sports. From December to April, ski-ing and skating events follow each other almost non-stop in nearly every mountain resort in

L

the country. Out of this tremendous range, perhaps the most notable are
as follows:

International Ladies' Ski Races, Grindelwald, early January.

International Lauberhorn Cup, Wengen, January.

Inferno Race, Mürren, February.

International Parsenn Derby, Davos, February.

Arlberg-Kandahar, the venue can vary each year, but it is frequently
held at Mürren, home of the Kandahar Ski Club, early in March.

There is no lack of spectator thrills, either, alongside the world famous
Cresta Run at St. Moritz, where several international competitions take
place every season amongst tobogganing enthusiasts.

Tour de Suisse, Zurich-back-to-Zurich (via about 1,000 miles),
starting mid-June. The route varies each year, but motorists in a hurry
should avoid it if they can! Crowds line the route through towns and
villages, and the cyclists have a fine supporting cast of cars and vans, most
of them advertising something and scattering free samples as they go.

Swiss Tennis Championships, Gstaad, end of July.

Knabenschiessen, Boys' Shooting Contest, Zurich, week-end
in September. Thousands of youths between the ages of 12 and 16 take
part in this contest whose origins go back to the Middle Ages. The third
day develops into a popular festival, when the young marksmen form a
procession and the "shooting king" is elected, with much general
festivity.

Federal Gymnastics Festival and **Federal Shooting Festival.**
The Swiss are great enthusiasts for both these pastimes, and nearly every
village has its shooting and gym societies. Regional contests take place
regularly, and, approximately every four years, a big Federal event draws
thousands of contestants.

TRADE FAIRS

International Motor Show, Geneva, March.

Swiss Industries Fair, Basle, April.

Watches and Jewels Exhibition, Geneva, September.

Comptoir Suisse, Lausanne, September.   The national autumn
fair at which a guest foreign country puts on a big display each year.

National Exhibition.   Last held in 1939, the next of Switzerland's
giant exhibitions will take place in Lausanne in 1964.

TRADITIONAL

Chalanda Marz Festival, villages in the Engadine valley, March 1st.
In days gone by, this ear splitting performance through the streets by
village boys with cow bells, gongs and other resounding instruments
served, not surprisingly, to frighten winter demons away. Today, the
boys are still rewarded by gifts from the villagers, probably thankful at

the prospect of a more peaceful afternoon ! The day includes a feast for all the school children. Best of the Chalanda Marz festivities are to be seen in the Oberhalbstein Valley. At Salux, festivities end with a vigorous rough-and-tumble as the boys go out to wage war on those of neighbouring villages.

Sechseläuten, Spring Ceremony of the Zurich Guilds, Zurich, Monday towards the end of April. A two-day celebration with processions of children and costumed guildsmen, climaxed by the burning of a symbolic snowman, known as Böögg, amidst much jubilation.

Landsgemeinde, Open Air Parliament, cantons of Glaris, Appenzell, Obwalden and Nidwalden, last Sunday in April or first Sunday in May. All the local male voters—women do not have the vote— gather to decide by a show of hands on any new legislation which is put before them. In Appenzell, the ceremony takes place on alternate years at Trogen or Hundwil. The ancient ritual begins as the magistrates in office, headed by their chief, the Landammann, arrive in the main square, preceded by the inevitable bands. Each voter present carries a sword as a symbol of his rights and freedom. In the olden days, this kind of parliament, in which discussion is open to everyone, was customary all over the country.

Ceremonial Driving of Cattle to Summer Alpine Pastures, in many mountain districts, usually from middle to end of June. Particularly picturesque above Alt-St. Johann and Urnäsch. In some parts of the Canton of Valais, cow fights are staged to decide which animals shall lead the herd. About mid-September, the cows are ceremoniously driven back to the valleys again.

Children's Festival, St. Gall, first Tuesday in July. The biggest of many such festivals which take place at the end of the summer school term, the one at St. Gall unfolds on alternate years (uneven numbers) with processions of school children in festive costume, carnival, sporting contests and dancing.

Swiss Federal Hornuss Festival, different venue each year. The festival is the main event for this very ancient game which is played all over the country, but mainly in the Canton of Berne. Very faintly reminiscent of cricket, the " batsman " must hit the " puck " with a mallet which has an elastic handle of ash wood about eight feet long. Fielders try and stop the puck by wielding rectangular wooden rackets which are frequently thrown into the air as the puck comes flying high above them. The excitement can become terrific amongst watching Hornussen fans.

Brünig Mountain-style Wrestling Festival, Brünig Pass, first or second Sunday in August. Yodelling and flag-throwing accompany this open air event, one of the two oldest of its kind. Similar wrestling festivals are held in many mountain centres in July and August.

Fête des Vignerons, Vevey, August, approximately every 25 years. This lovely pageant of music, ballet and song depicting the passage of the seasons through the vineyards takes place in an open air theatre, specially built each time on the market place against the backdrop of the Lake of Geneva and the mountains beyond. Internationally known stars take the leading parts, but the supporting cast of thousands is drawn from the population of this pleasant little wine-growing town. It was last held in 1955.

Klausjagen, Traditional Appearance of St. Nicholas, Central Switzerland, December 4th to 6th. The most elaborate procession takes place at Küssnacht, where Santa Claus is followed by dancers wearing gigantic headgear made of cardboard and lit from within by candles. At Zurich, on December 6th, several hundred children take part in the Wollishofer Kläuse procession, wearing high lantern hats and making a good deal of noise on a variety of instruments.

Swiss Costumes Festival, different place and time each year.

WINE AND FOOD FESTIVALS

Grape Harvest Festival, Neuchâtel, last Sunday in September or first Sunday in October. A rich procession of floral floats is followed by confetti fights, dancing and various entertainments in the evening.

Grape Harvest Procession, Lugano, last Sunday in September or first Sunday in October.

CHAPTER TWENTY-SEVEN

Turkey

EUROPE MEETS ASIA ON THE SHORES OF THE BOSPHORUS AND THE Dardanelles, and though only about 3 per cent. of Turkey's land area qualifies as Europe, a number of the more important events have been included for the rest of the country as well.

Spring is a glorious time in this vast country caught between the Aegean, the Mediterranean and the Black Sea, and during the period of April to June, Turkey holds several of her many patriotic festivals, as well as her main trade fair, an unusual sporting event and a drama festival in exceptional surroundings.

CULTURAL EVENTS

Spring Festival, Aspendos (formerly Belkis), usually late April or early May. Tucked away in southern Turkey, there's a superb and virtually undeveloped riviera. Its main centre is Antalya, and 30 miles from there, in the village of Aspendos, students of the State Conservatory in Ankara come every spring to stage classical plays in an ancient Greek amphitheatre. If you like archaeology, the whole of this area abounds in the ruins of Greek civilisations, barely touched yet by the experts. A little difficult to reach, but infinitely worth the effort.

NATIONAL OR SPECIAL DAYS

January 6th. On this day in 1961, the Constituent Assembly met for the first time, after the revolution in May, 1960. This has been established as a national holiday in future years.

Children's Day, throughout the country, April 23rd. Commemorating the inauguration of the National Assembly in 1920, this is principally a day for the youngsters. Elected representatives from schools in Ankara are received by the President and his family, and in places children may well benefit by free seats in cinemas, free taxi rides and ice cream ! A festive day for young people, both in public and in private.

May Day, throughout the country, May 1st. Though technically following the tradition of Labour Movements all over the world, in Turkey this is largely an occasion for picnics *en famille*.

May 19th, throughout the country. On this day in 1919, Kemal Atatürk landed at Samsun and began the great national movement for independence. To mark the occasion, young athletes bear a burning torch from Samsun to the capital, and sporting events are held in main centres.

May 27th. This anniversary of the victory of the Reform Movement in 1960 will undoubtedly become an annual occasion for celebration in future years.

Victory Day, throughout the country, August 30th. Big military parades in Ankara by the Turkish armed forces mark Turkish victory in the War of Independence in 1923.

Republic Day, throughout the country, October 29th. Parades, music, torchlight processions and general festivity honour the proclamation of the First Turkish Republic on this day in 1923. This public holiday lasts for two days.

November 10th. A two-minute silence at 9.5 a.m. pays homage to the memory of Kemal Atatürk, who died on November 10th, 1938.

RELIGIOUS EVENTS

Seker Bayram and **Kurban Bayram,** throughout the country. The majority of Turks follow the Moslem faith, and these are the two most important of their religious festivals. The dates vary considerably each year, according to the Moslem Calendar. On the occasion of Seker Bayram, gifts of sweets, handkerchiefs, etc., are exchanged (*Seker* means " sugar "); Kurban Bayram is the more serious of the two festivals (*Kurban* means " sacrifice "), recalling symbolically Abraham's sacrifice to Allah. On this occasion, sheep are sacrificed, and the meat distributed to the poor.

Christian Festivals. A substantial Christian following remains largely in Istanbul and the surrounding area. The majority of Christian adherents follow the Greek Orthodox faith, and the Orthodox Patriarchate is at the church at Fener on the Golden Horn. Principal Christian festivals in Turkey are:

Feast of Epiphany, January 6th. A Blessing of the Waters ceremony is held on the shores of the Bosphorus on the promontory of Akintiburnu, between the resorts of Bebek and Arnavutköy. Men dive into the sea for the golden cross.

Orthodox Day, first Sunday in Lent. Marked by colourful ceremonies at the church at Fener.

Easter Sunday. According to the Orthodox calendar, this always falls on the first Sunday after the full moon following the spring equinox. A brilliant ceremony takes place at the church at Fener.

St. Andrew's Day, November 30th. A special ceremony honours St. Andrew, who founded the church at Fener.

Pilgrimages. At the house of Panaya Kapulu near Ephesus, it is said that the Virgin Mary spent some of the last days of her life. The house is now a chapel and has recently been restored. Authenticated by the Roman Catholic Church, this has become a popular place of pilgrimage.

SPORTING FIXTURES

Turkish Wrestling Championships, Kirkpinar, end of May or early June. Turkish skill in wrestling has been proved at many an Olympic Games. They have, too, their own national form of the sport, in which oil is smeared over the bodies of the contestants and on their leather knee breeches. It's a slippery business requiring exceptional skill— and training to develop strength of grip. Scene of the annual championships is at the village of Kirkpinar, near Edirne (formerly Adrianople) near the Turkish-Greek border.

TRADE FAIRS

International Izmir Trade Fair, Izmir, August 20th to September 20th. Nearly 2,000,000 visitors have attended the event in previous years; it features pavilions of 20 different countries.

CHAPTER TWENTY-EIGHT

Yugoslavia

THOUGH YUGOSLAVIA'S MOST IMPORTANT CULTURAL EVENT, THE Dubrovnik Summer Festival, takes place during the peak holiday weeks of July and August, my recommendation—culture apart—is the month of May for the gloriously warm days of late Spring. In May, too, perhaps the greatest of Yugoslavia's national celebrations takes place—the Day of Youth, in honour of Marshal Tito's birthday on May 25th. On this day and during the period preceding it, echoes of these nation-wide festivities can be heard in towns and villages, from the rugged mountain ranges to the vast plains and forests of this beautiful country.

AGRICULTURAL, HORTICULTURAL AND LIVESTOCK SHOWS

International Agricultural Fair, Novi Sad, end of April to early May.

CARNIVALS

Split Carnival, February.   Three days of merrymaking, with colourful costumes much in evidence.

CULTURAL EVENTS

Dubrovnik Summer Festival, Dubrovnik, early July to third week in August.   This is undoubtedly the highlight of Yugoslavia's cultural activities, in which high quality of performance combines with superb natural settings in this medieval town on the shores of the Adriatic. Opera, ballet, music, drama and folk dancing programmes include internationally known names from a variety of countries.

International Biennal Festival of Contemporary Music, Zagreb, late May.

Split Summer Festival, Split, mid August. Opera, ballet, music and drama.

Ljubjana Festival, Ljubjana, ten days in July. Music, dancing, art and handicrafts. Also **Festival of Films.**

Festival of Yugoslav Films, Pula, August. The best of Yugoslavia's films are shown in the unusual setting of the Roman arena.

NATIONAL OR SPECIAL DAYS

International Labour Day, all over the country, May 1st. Celebrations include parades of every kind, sporting events and folk dancing, and can be seen at their best in Belgrade or, on a lesser scale, at Ljubjana, Sarajevo, Skoplje, Titograd and Zagreb.

Anniversary of the National Revolution, July 4th, with celebrations in Belgrade, Titivo and Užice.

Day of Youth, all over the country, May 25th. Every Yugoslav contributes to this monumental birthday celebration for Marshal Tito, who has turned the occasion into a national festival of youth. Anything up to two weeks beforehand, youthful runners set out from remote villages all over the country, bearing messages to Belgrade. Messages pass from hand to hand, rather as in a marathon relay race, until they pour in their thousands into Belgrade on the appointed day. Sporting contests, cultural events and folk dances take place all over the country during this period, culminating in big festivities in Belgrade itself. The whole operation is an example of team work on a national scale.

SPORTING FIXTURES

International Fair of Marine Tourism and Fishing, Zadar, early July. Various touristic, cultural and scientific events include trips by special fishing boats to some of the excellent fishing grounds nearby— with entertainment provided.

Regatta, Lošinj, mid-August.

Regatta, Rijeka, early September.

TRADE FAIRS

International Trade Fair, Zagreb, held twice a year in the spring and autumn. This is the most important event of its kind in Yugoslavia.

International Tobacco Fair, Skoplje, early September.

TRADITIONAL CUSTOMS

Traditional Wedding Celebrations, Galičnik, July 12th. Most colourful mass weddings in traditional costume take place on this day, when the men who have left the village to work in nearby towns, or even further afield, return to be married. Numbers, naturally, vary considerably from year to year, but Galičnik is the last stronghold of this ancient custom.

Moreska, Traditional Play, Korčula, July 27th. A colourful pageant commemorating former struggles between the Turks and the Moors.

Sarajevo Folklore Festival, Sarajevo, end of July to end of August. The best of many annual events featuring folk song, dance and costume.

Sinjska Alka, Traditional Knightly Tournament, Sinj, August.

Traditional ceremonies and jousting contests open with a costumed parade of the Sinj, who drove the Turks from Dalmatia.

Folklore Festivals, resorts in Istria, early August.

Cow-Ball Festival, Bohinj, late September, on the occasion of the return of the herds from the mountains.

WINE AND FOOD FESTIVALS

Carnival of Grapes, Smederevo, end of September to early October. Processions, dancing and general merrymaking are undoubtedly stimulated by the wine which, on this occasion, literally flows from the taps in this little town not far from Belgrade !

Directory

Austrian State Tourist Department, 219 Regent Street, London, W.1.

Belgian National Tourist Office, 167 Regent Street, W.1.

British Travel Association, 64 St. James's Street, S.W.1.

Cyprus Government Office, 168 Regent Street, W.1.

National Travel Association of Denmark, 2 Conduit Street, W.1.

Finnish Travel Information Centre, 56 Haymarket, S.W.1.

French Government Tourist Office, 66 Haymarket, S.W.1,
  also at 20 Upper Fitzwilliam Street, Dublin.

German Tourist Information Bureau, 61 Conduit Street, W.1.

Greek Tourist Office, 195 Regent Street, W.1.

Netherlands National Tourist Office, 38 Hyde Park Gate, S.W.7.

Iceland Tourist Information Bureau, 161 Piccadilly, W.1.

Irish Tourist Office, 71 Regent Street, W.1.

Italian State Tourist Department, 201 Regent Street, W.1.

Liechtenstein Tourist Office, Vaduz, Liechtenstein.

Luxembourg National Tourist Office, 167 Regent Street, W.1.

Dept. of Tourism, Malta Government Office, 24 Haymarket, S.W.1.

Norwegian National Tourist Office, 20 Pall Mall, S.W.1.

Portuguese Tourist Office, 20 Lower Regent Street, S.W.1.

Scottish Tourist Board, Rutland Place, Edinburgh, 1.

Spanish National Tourist Office, 67 Jermyn Street, S.W.1.

Swedish National Tourist Office, 52-53 Conduit Street, W.1.

Swiss National Tourist Office, 458 Strand, W.C.2.

Turkey Tourist Department, 43 Belgrave Square, S.W.1.

Yugoslav National Tourist Office, 143 Regent Street, W.1.

Index

NORWAY  NORWAY

Bergen
International Festival

ROYAL PATRON: His Majesty King Olav V

May-June

MUSIC · DRAMA · FOLKLORE

An annual Festival of sound and colour · 60-70 concerts
and performances · Internationally known artists and
orchestras · Recitals in the home of Edvard Grieg
Drama by Henrik Ibsen · Norwegian Folklore programme.

★

Further information from The Bergen International Festival, Bergen, Norway, or
Norwegian National Tourist Office, 20 Pall Mall, London S.W.1. Tel: TRA 6255